Wealth Management

Wealth Management

Erik Lie

BEP

BUSINESS EXPERT PRESS

Leader in applied, concise business books

Wealth Management

Cover design by Eloy Sánchez-Vizcaíno Mengual

Interior design by Exeter Premedia Services Private Ltd., Chennai, India

First published in 2023 by
Business Expert Press, LLC
222 East 46th Street, New York, NY 10017
www.businessexpertpress.com

ISBN-13: 978-1-63742-522-0 (paperback)
ISBN-13: 978-1-63742-523-7 (e-book)

Business Expert Press Finance and Financial Management Collection

First edition: 2023

10 9 8 7 6 5 4 3 2 1

Description

This book empowers individuals with *practical knowledge to manage their financial wealth from their first job until retirement and beyond.*

The first main theme is **investments** and covers security types, investment strategies, and asset allocations for individual investors. The foundation for this theme is the magical behavior of investment returns across securities and time and the concept of market efficiency.

Next, the author discusses **tax minimization**, beginning with an understanding of how taxes deplete investment value. He then illuminates various tax loopholes and strategies that individuals can exploit, including:

- The use of tax-favored investment accounts;
- Opportunistic trading;
- Picking ETFs over mutual funds;
- Gifting to bypass estate taxes.

Lie also covers the many **pitfalls** in the world of wealth management. Several stem from investors' ignorance or irrational behavior, while others are concocted by financial institutions to fleece individual investors. Either way, the readers learn to avoid them.

Other topics include:

- What types of insurance should individuals purchase?
- When should a mortgage be refinanced?
- And how can individuals avoid costly probate court for the estate?

This book is useful for university courses on wealth management and for *all individuals who want to secure their financial future.* **This includes you.**

Keywords

wealth management; investments; retirement accounts; mutual funds; insurance; taxes; estate planning

Contents

Acknowledgments

Thanks to Melanie Alexander, Randy Heron, John Lewis, Elaheh Seyed Alikhani, John Spitzer, and Ashish Tiwari for helpful comments on earlier drafts. Special thanks to Eloy Sánchez-Vizcaíno Mengual for superb illustrations.

CHAPTER 1

Introduction

I initially wrote this book as a textbook for a wealth management class with students who already had some basic knowledge of finance. But the vast portion of the material is suitable for a broader audience with no finance background. And while the book contains some finance theory and math, it is intended to be very practical, and you can skip most of the math with limited loss of the content.

The book is not a personal finance book for dummies. I am not going to tell you to pay off your credit card balance every month or that you should never borrow from a payday lender. I assume you already know that. But I will not go to the other extreme either, by reviewing, say, short selling (which you should stay away from) or the valuation of securities (which is a futile exercise for individuals not working on Wall Street).

It has taken me a long time to discover and digest the material in this book. I thought I was quite educated in financial matters when I got my PhD, but I was very wrong. I wish I had known the content in this book at an earlier stage of my career so that I could have made wiser financial decisions. In any event, I want to pass on the content to others who are in their early stages because the earlier you know the lessons in this book and adopt them, the better your financial health will be later. But even if you are already well into your career or close to retirement, you should benefit greatly.

Figure 1.1 provides a simplistic overview of some basic principles in this book. The surest path to wealth in the long run (beyond the obvious of saving as much as you can) is to (i) fully exploit retirement accounts and other tax-advantaged accounts and (ii) place most of the money in the stock market using low-fee exchange-traded funds and individual stocks. You should also supplement with investments in regular brokerage accounts (though these investments require some extra tax maneuvering) and basic insurance products, including health insurance and term life

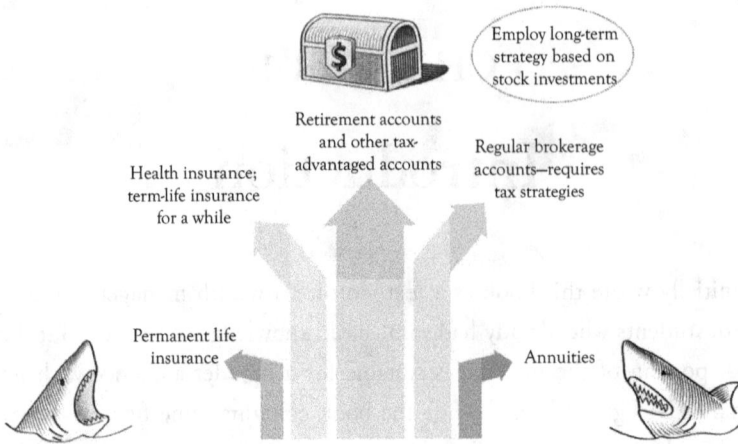

Figure 1.1 Overview of some basic principles

insurance, while you have dependents. In contrast, I argue that use of permanent life insurance products and annuities should be limited. Oh— the sharks represent anyone who wants a bite of your wealth, including insurance salespeople, financial advisers, and tax collectors, though this, of course, is an overdramatization.

The book helps you navigate the pitfalls and opportunities in the world of wealth management. I will also express my personal opinions in places. But I am not a lawyer, and you should seek legal advice if you encounter complex legal uncertainties and challenges.

You might also want to consult a financial adviser on occasion as a supplement to this book. There is an abundance of individuals who call themselves financial advisers and planners, so you should ensure that the adviser is a *fiduciary*, meaning that (s)he is obligated to act in your best interest.[1] You might even request a written confirmation that (s)he

---

[1] In 2020, the Securities and Exchange Commission (SEC) adopted the *Regulation Best Interest* (Reg BI) for brokers and investment advisers. Reg BI is an improvement from the earlier *suitability* standard, requiring that advisers only recommend so-called *suitable* investments, that is, investments that suit the client's goals and risk tolerance, even if they have high commissions. Yet, experts generally agree that Reg BI does not protect clients as well as the fiduciary standard. For example, if you sue your adviser for bad advice, a fiduciary adviser must prove that the advice was in your best interest, whereas as a nonfiduciary adviser can leave the burden of proof to you.

is a fiduciary before proceeding. A safe choice is a Registered Investment Adviser (RIA) because RIAs must act as fiduciaries and are registered with the Securities and Exchange Commission (SEC) or state regulatory agencies. Furthermore, I recommend that you pay a flat or hourly rate for the services. I believe that advisers who earn commissions or trading fees have perverse incentives to recommend inappropriate products and excessive trading, and those who charge a fraction of clients' assets under management (AUM) end up being more expensive for the clients than they should be. For example, five hours of service might cost you 5 hours × $200 = $1,000, whereas a 1 percent fee on a portfolio of half a million dollars amounts to 1% × $500,000 = $5,000 *annually*.

If you keep on reading, you will make better financial decisions and be less reliant on outside help. Both should enhance your financial resilience, and perhaps even happiness, in the long run.

CHAPTER 2

Investment Returns and Investment Principles

As an individual investor, you have access to many different types of investments, ranging from education (which is an investment in your human capital) to shares in publicly traded companies (i.e., stocks). What matters for investors is the *return* over time from those investments. This chapter reviews the calculation and behavior of returns. The focus is on returns on investments in stocks and bonds, which form the basis for much of our wealth accumulation, while later chapters cover real estate and various insurance products.

The main objectives for this chapter are:

- Explore investment returns of stocks and bonds, including how returns behave across securities and time.
- Learn some basic investment principles based on the aforementioned exploration, including the benefits of:
  o Diversification across many securities; and
  o Investing in riskier securities for longer investment horizons.

Investment Returns

Figure 2.1 shows the calculation of the return on investment. This investment return can be highly uncertain, and we often refer to that uncertainty as *volatility* and measure it with standard deviation. Importantly, most of the volatility stems from the first part of the investment return, that is, the capital gain. The second part, that is, the return from capital distributions, is much more stable and predictable in practice.

$$\text{Investment return} = \frac{\overbrace{\text{End price} - \text{Beginning price}}^{\text{Capital gain (or loss)}}}{\text{Beginning price}} + \frac{\text{Cash distributions from the security}}{\text{Beginning price}}$$

Volatile   Stable

Figure 2.1 Calculation of investment return

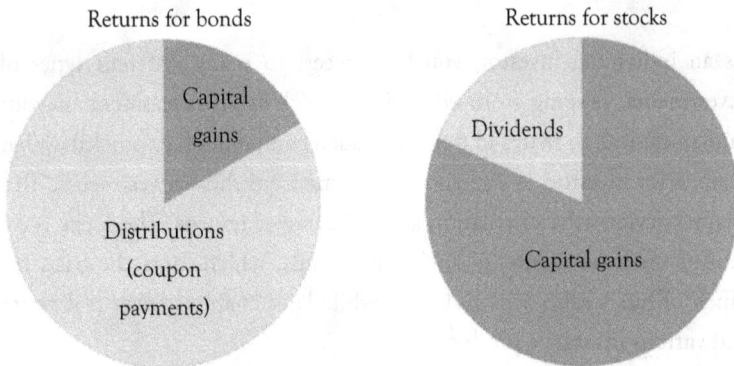

Returns for bonds   Returns for stocks

Capital gains

Dividends

Distributions (coupon payments)

Capital gains

Figure 2.2 The sources of returns for bonds and stocks

The relative magnitudes of the two sources of returns, capital gains and distributions, differ greatly across securities, as illustrated in Figure 2.2. Bonds get most of their return from distributions (i.e., interest payments), while stocks get most of their return from capital gains and only a modest return from distributions (i.e., dividends). Furthermore, the capital gains for bonds from issuance to maturity is set. Thus, bond returns are less volatile than stock returns. The next subsections discuss these issues in greater detail.

Bonds and Bond Returns

Bonds are debt securities issued by the federal government (Treasury bills and bonds), state and local governments (municipal bonds, or *munis*), and corporations. You can readily buy individual Treasury bills and bonds. However, the markets for individual munis and corporate bonds are rather illiquid, making purchases expensive, just like buying foreign currency from a street vendor. Thus, if you wish to invest in bonds, you are likely better off buying some mutual fund or exchange-traded fund

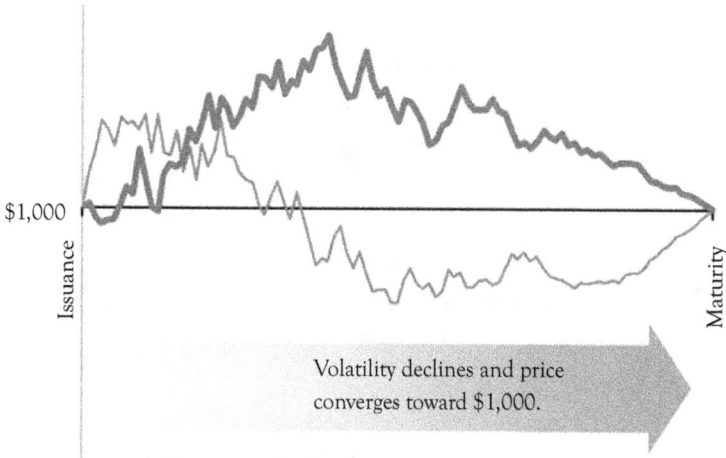

Figure 2.3 Bond prices over time

(ETF) that specializes in bonds, such as Vanguard's total bond market ETF (with ticker symbol BND).

Most bonds pay periodic interest payments, also called coupons, typically every 6 or 12 months. The primary return from buying bonds stems from these coupon payments. However, it is also possible for an investor who does not hold a bond from issuance to maturity to experience considerable capital gain or loss because bond prices fluctuate over time.

This book will not cover bond valuation because there is no need for most individual investors to have that skill. Yet it is useful to know how bonds change in value between issuance and maturity.

Figure 2.3 shows the price over time for two hypothetical bonds with the common par value of $1,000.[1] There are several noteworthy aspects:

1. The prices around the issuance are very close to the bond's par value of $1,000.[2]

2. The prices fluctuate after the issue because either the interest rates in the market change or the credit risk of the issuer changes. In the

---

[1] The graph presents so-called *clean* bond prices, which exclude accrued interest between coupon payments that typically occur every six months.

[2] For those who are curious, this occurs because the issuer sets the *coupon rate*, that is, the annual coupons scaled by the par value, to be roughly equal to the *bond yield*, that is, the return that investors expect on the bond. That way, investors expect to get their entire return in the form of coupon payments.

graph, the bond prices increased in the early life of both bonds, meaning that either the general interest rates or the credit risk of the issuer decreased. However, the bond price of one of the bonds decreased leading up to the middle of its life because of an increase in interest rates or credit risk.

3. As the bonds mature, the price fluctuations subside, and the price approaches $1,000, right where it started. This shows that an investor who buys the bonds upon issuance and holds them to maturity experiences no price gain or loss, and the entire investment return comes as coupon payments.

There are also some bonds that do not pay coupons, so-called *zero-coupon bonds*. Most prominent of these are Treasury bills, which have such short maturity (from three months to a year) that coupons do not make sense. Because they lack coupons, they will be trading at a discount relative to their par value, which is why they are called *discount bonds* (along with other bonds that trade at a discount relative to their par value). Figure 2.4 shows a typical price path for a zero-coupon bond, starting well below the par value and slowly increasing toward the par value as it matures.

Zero-coupon bonds are unique in that they expect to yield their entire return in the form of capital gain. However, this capital gain from the issuance to maturity is perfectly predictable (though the exact path is not). Furthermore, investors must report a pro-rated portion as interest for tax purposes. That means that even zero-coupon bonds are deemed to have most of their return as coupons.

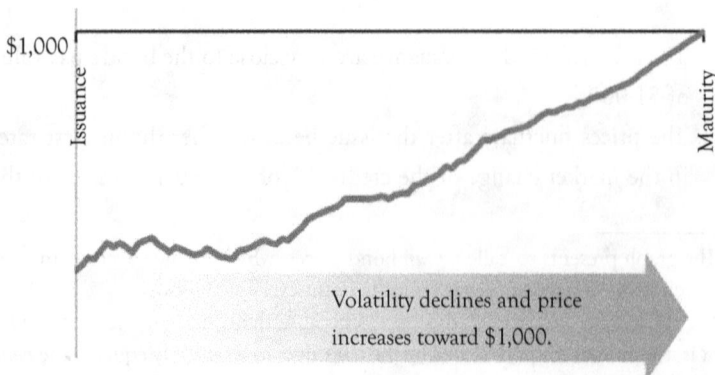

Figure 2.4 Zero-coupon bond prices over time

The key takeaway then is that, at least for tax purposes, *bonds get most of their return from coupon payments*, while the capital gains and losses tend to be moderate. A later chapter discusses how the coupons and capital gains are taxed.

Stocks and Stock Returns

Stocks (shares) represent ownership in a company. As a shareholder, you have certain rights, including the right to vote on who will represent you on the board of directors and the right to partake in any cash distributions to shareholders, that is, dividends. Thus, the investment return from holding a stock comes from capital gain (or loss) and the *dividend yield*, that is, the annual dividend scaled by the stock price. Both the expected capital gain and the dividend yield vary substantially across individual stocks and sectors. For example, stocks in high-tech companies tend not to pay any dividends at all, but they are expected to produce high capital gain. Conversely, companies in mature and stable industries, for example, utilities, tend to pay large dividends and are expected to produce modest capital gain.

In the aggregate, the capital gain of publicly traded companies in the United States far exceeds the dividend yield. For example, the average dividend yield for S&P 500 companies hovers around 2 percent (and it is less for smaller companies), whereas the capital gain has historically been four to five times greater. Figure 2.5 shows the possible evolution

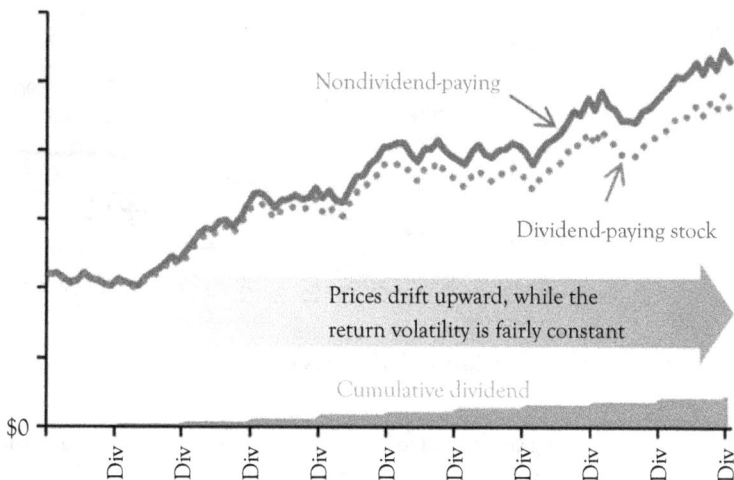

Figure 2.5 Stock prices over time

of stock prices over time if we assume either no dividends or a modest dividend paid on the days denoted on the X-axis. You can see that (i) the prices tend to drift upward, (ii) the price gain is stronger when there is no dividend, and (iii) the volatility of returns is fairly constant over time, though it might decrease very slowly as the companies get sufficiently large and mature.

Importantly, dividends have no effect on the total investment return in this simple framework, in that firms with a higher dividend yield have a correspondingly lower capital gain. That does not mean that dividends are irrelevant for investors; capital gains and dividends are taxed differently, which affects our optimal choice of dividend-paying versus nondividend-paying stocks.[3] I will return to this in the next chapter.

The Historical Record

It is informative to examine the historical record of bonds and stocks to get a sense of their levels and volatilities of returns. Figure 2.6 shows what would have happened over time to a one-dollar investment in 1927 in either Treasury bills, Treasury bonds, corporate bonds with a bond rating of *Baa* (i.e., corporate bonds with modest credit risk), or S&P 500 stocks. The depicted returns capture both capital gains (losses) and

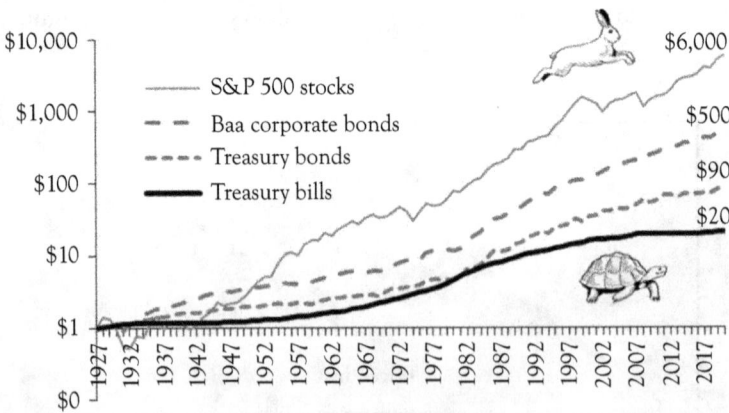

Figure 2.6 The historical record of stocks and bonds

---

[3] Also, dividend-paying stocks tend to be less volatile, not because of the dividend per se but because less volatile companies choose to pay higher dividends.

cash distributions. The y-axis is logarithmic so that you can better see the action throughout the entire period; otherwise, you would barely be able to see the price movements in the earlier period.

What can we learn from the graph? The investment in Treasury bills is the tortoise in the graph, with its slow and steady appreciation. By 2020, the investment was worth $20, and it never slipped much, even during the 1929 crash, the burst of the tech bubble in 2000, and the 2008 financial crisis. In contrast, the investment in the S&P 500 stocks is the hare, with remarkable overall performance, despite some dormant periods and occasional setbacks. By 2000, the one-dollar investment in the S&P 500 had turned into a whopping $6,000. Thus, in this race, the hare clearly won. The Treasury bonds and corporate bonds fall in between the Treasury bills and S&P 500 stocks.

I also calculated the average and standard deviation of the returns for each of the four investments and made a graph of these simple statistics, as depicted in Figure 2.7. The S&P 500 stocks not only had the highest standard deviation but also the highest average return. On the other end of the spectrum, the Treasury bills had the lowest standard deviation and the lowest average return. The Treasury bonds and corporate bonds are in the middle along both dimensions. Based on this, we can generalize by stating that *higher volatility is associated with higher return*. This generalization is one of the important building blocks in finance and holds for groups of securities (i.e., portfolios). The implication is that

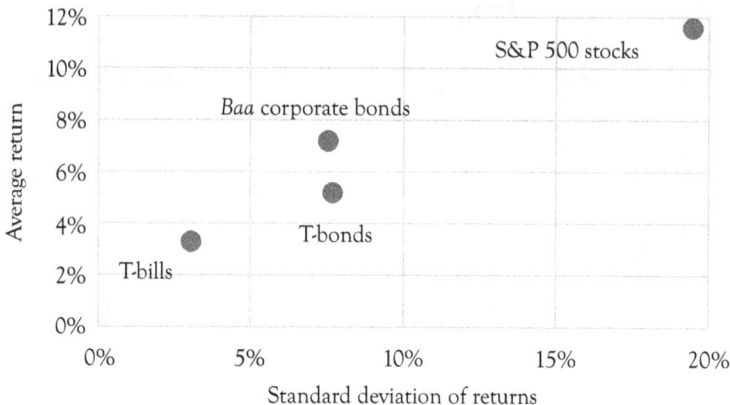

Figure 2.7 Standard deviation versus average return

investors are compensated for taking on risk. Later, we will make some modifications for individual securities by partitioning the volatility into two types.

You might wonder why the Treasury bonds have greater volatility than Treasury bills, given that they are both issued by the U.S. Treasury and are considered to be free of credit risk. If you recall from the discussion of bond prices over time, the volatility decreases as we got closer to maturity because changes in interest rates are less consequential when bonds are about to mature. That further implies that long-term bonds have greater volatility than short-term bonds, which explains why Treasury bills, with their time to maturity of a maximum of one year, have lower volatility than Treasury bonds.

Likewise, despite their higher credit risk, corporate bonds have similar volatility as Treasury bonds because corporate bonds tend to have lower time to maturity. But you could argue that this is a bit deceptive. If an investor holds Treasury bonds from issuance to maturity, the return is certain. In contrast, if an investor holds corporate bonds from issuance to maturity, the return might be uncertain to the extent that it is unclear whether the corporation can pay off its debt. That could explain why corporate bonds have a higher average return.

Even if you got a bit lost in the preceding discussion, just remember the key takeaway from this section: *the riskier your investment portfolio is, the higher the return you can expect.*

The Magic of Sigma

We use the Greek symbol sigma (σ) to denote the standard deviation, and in the context of investments, the standard deviation is based on the returns. Henceforth, I use both sigma and volatility to mean the standard deviation of returns. It turns out that sigma has two special—I would even venture to say magical—properties, as Figure 2.8 illustrates. We will see that these properties have crucial implications for our investment strategies. Many find this topic to be fascinating. Others find it overly technical. If you are in the latter group, you may skip ahead to the next section that describes investment implications. I promise no hard feelings if you do so.

Figure 2.8 The magic of sigma

The Diminishing Sigma When Combining Securities

The first magical property is what happens when we combine securities into portfolios. Before we get there, let us see what happens to the expected return for a portfolio with two securities: (i) security a with expected return of $E(r_a)$ and proportion invested of w_a, and (ii) security b with expected return of $E(r_b)$ and proportion invested of w_b. The expected return for a portfolio p is then $w_a \times E(r_a) + w_b \times E(r_b)$. For example, if we invest 50 percent in security a with an expected return of 4 and 50 percent in security b with an expected return of 8 percent, the expected portfolio return is simply $50\% \times 4\% + 50\% \times 8\% = 6\%$, that is, dead in the middle of the expected returns of the two securities. This is a *linear* function.

The calculation of the standard deviation of the portfolio is trickier. It turns out that the variance (i.e., the standard deviation squared) of the portfolio can be expressed as $(w_a\sigma_a)^2 + (w_b\sigma_b)^2 + 2(w_a\sigma_a)(w_b\sigma_b)\rho_{a,b}$, where σ_a is the standard deviation for security a, σ_b is the standard deviation for security b, and $\rho_{a,b}$ is the correlation between the returns of securities a and b. For example, if the standard deviations for securities a and b are 20 and 40 percent and the correlation of the returns is 50 percent, the variance of our portfolio is $(0.5 \times 0.2)^2 + (0.5 \times 0.4)^2 + 2(0.5 \times 0.2)$ $(0.5 \times 0.4)0.5 = 0.07$, and the standard deviation is $\sqrt{0.07} = 0.265$. Note that this is *lower* than the midpoint of the standard deviations of the two securities. Figure 2.9 plots the standard deviations and expected returns for the two securities and the portfolio of 50 percent in each. Because the standard deviation of the portfolio is below the midpoint for the two

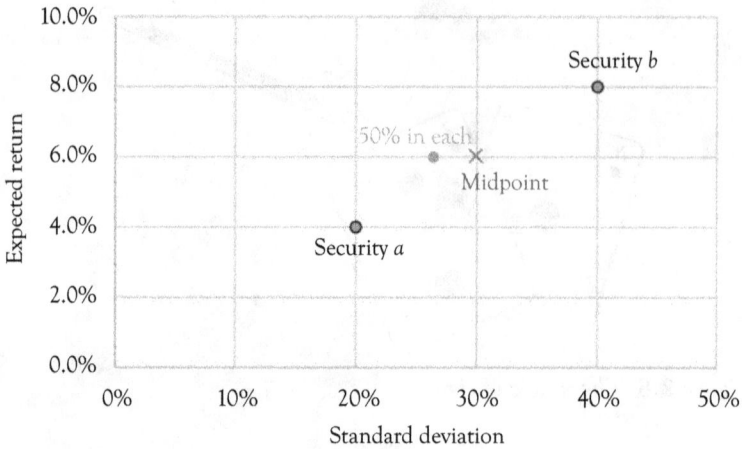

Figure 2.9 Two securities and a portfolio with 50 percent in each

securities, the location of the portfolio is *not* midway between the locations of the two securities.

I also calculated the expected returns and standard deviations for various portfolios with uneven weights on the two securities and plotted them in Figure 2.10. The plot shows that the combinations form a curved line between the two securities.

The curvature stems from the imperfect correlation between the two securities. Let me prove this by trying out other correlations, ranging

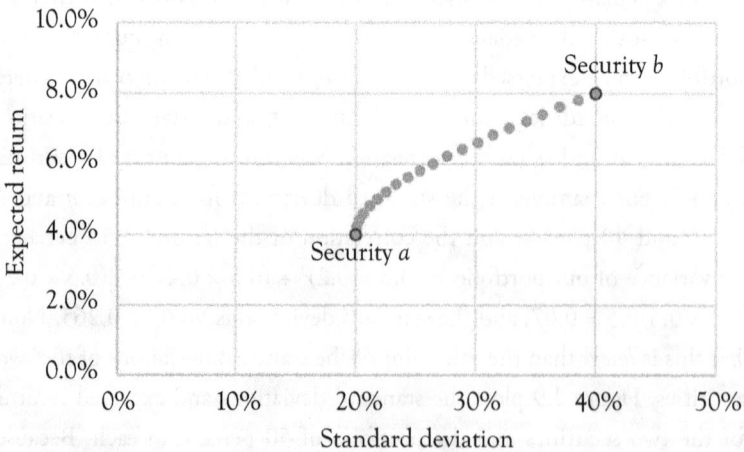

Figure 2.10 Portfolios based on two securities

from perfect negative correlation ($\rho_{a,b} = -1$) to perfect positive correlation ($\rho_{a,b} = +1$). Figure 2.11 shows the results. With perfect positive correlation, the portfolios form a straight line between the two securities. But as the correlation drops, the magic emerges. In fact, with sufficiently low correlations, there are portfolios with smaller standard deviation than either of the standard deviations of the individual securities. With a perfect negative correlation, it is even possible to create a portfolio with no risk by investing 2/3 in security a and 1/3 in security b. You must agree that making the risk disappear like this is pure magic.

We have seen that in the special case when the returns of two securities are perfectly correlated ($\rho = 1$), combinations of the two securities have expected returns and standard deviations that are just weighted averages of those of the two securities, thus forming a straight line when we make a plot. However, this is highly unlikely to occur in practice.[4] In all other cases, there is a benefit in constructing portfolios of the two securities, in that some of the risk evaporates, and more so as the correlation falls. This tendency for risk to evaporate when combining securities continues as we add even more securities to our portfolio. Consider the three securities in Figure 2.12, which have realistic correlations of returns between 0.40 and 0.62.

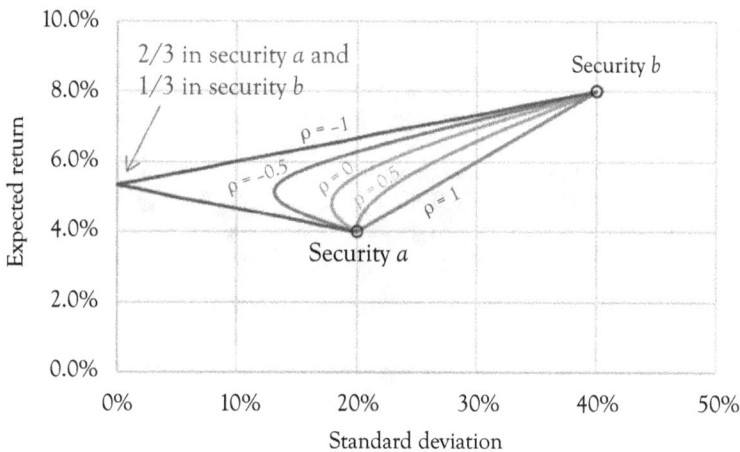

Figure 2.11 *Portfolios of two securities with various correlations*

---

[4] Another special case that forms a line is when one of the securities is risk-free, that is, the standard deviation of returns is zero. I will return to that later.

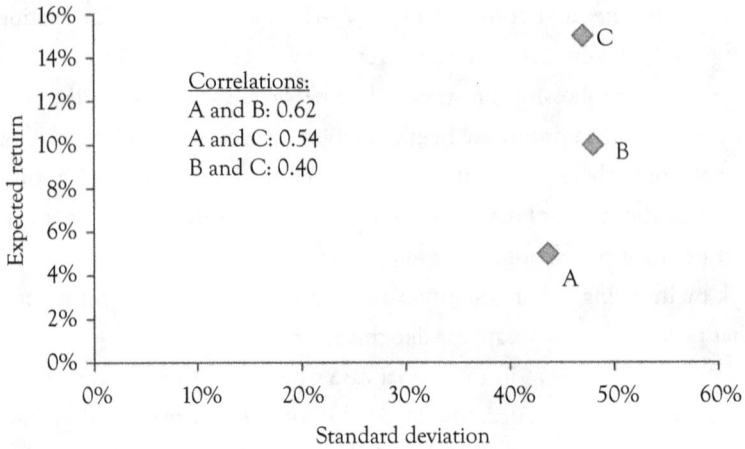

Figure 2.12 Standard deviation and expected return of three securities

First, we form portfolios of securities A and B. Those portfolios are emphasized in Figure 2.13 and have the same curvature we saw earlier. Next, we form portfolios of either securities B and C or securities A and C, and again we get some curvature. Finally, I tried combinations of all three securities, and we can attain even lower standard deviations. Indeed, the portfolio with the lowest standard deviation combine all three securities (about 30 percent in A, 30 percent in B, and 40 percent in C).

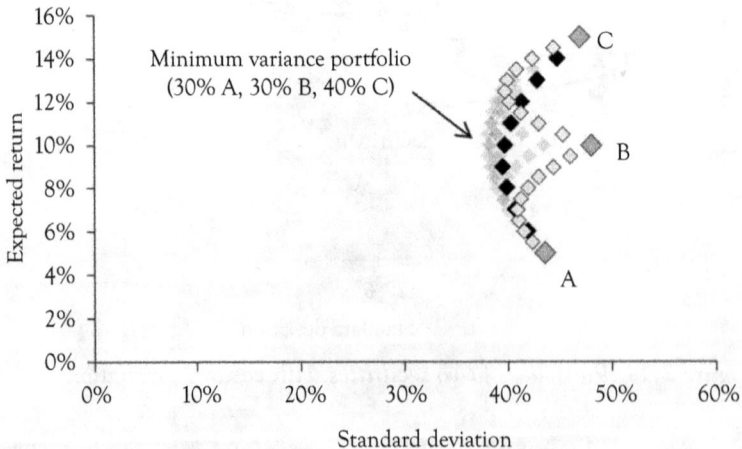

Figure 2.13 Portfolios of three securities

Figure 2.14 Do not put all your eggs in the same basket

In sum, we can reduce risk by combining securities in portfolios, and the reduction is more pronounced if (a) the securities have low correlations and (b) we use many securities. The implication is that *we should hold portfolios of many securities from widely different sectors.* As the saying goes: Do not put all your eggs in one basket, as Figure 2.14 illustrates.

Incidentally, when assessing whether you have too many eggs in one basket, you should also consider your income stream from your employment as an asset (or egg, if you will). For many, that income stream represents their most valuable asset, and other investments should therefore differ substantially. The implication is that if, say, you work for Apple, you should limit your investment in Apple stock and rather invest relatively more in nontech sectors. Just ask all the employees of Enron who had invested their retirement savings in the company upon the encouragement of the management team—when Enron collapsed, these people lost both their valuable jobs and their nest eggs.

The Fading Importance of Sigma Over Time

If you want to estimate the return across n periods, you cannot simply add the returns across the periods. Rather, you must calculate the return for n periods as $(1 + r_1) \times (1 + r_2) \times \ldots \times (1 + r_n) - 1$, which simplifies to

$(1 + r)^n - 1$, if the returns are the same in each period. Thus, if you invest in a security over two years at an annual interest of 10 percent, the total return is *not* $10\% \times 2 = 20\%$ but rather $(1 + 10\%)^2 - 1 = 21\%$. The extra 1 percent is interest on interest or *compound interest*. Compound interest causes investments to grow exponentially in value, and Albert Einstein dubbed it the eighth wonder of the world: "Compound interest is the eighth wonder of the world. He who understands it, earns it, he who doesn't, pays it."

The compounding effect of the expected return is widely recognized and an important reason for why you should start saving as early as possible. I am sure you have heard this advice many times already. What is not as widely recognized is the behavior of the standard deviation of returns over time. The *variance* is additive over time, meaning that the variance for n periods is simply the sum of the variances for each period. If the variances in each of the n periods are all the same at σ^2, the total variance for all periods is simply $\sigma^2 \times n$ and the total standard deviation is $\sigma\sqrt{n}$. This implies that the standard deviation of returns increases over time, as I am sure you expected, but the increase is decreasing over time. In other words, the increase in risk over time is surprisingly modest.

Let us combine these findings. Figure 2.15 depicts the expected return of 10 percent per year over time (which is increasing at an

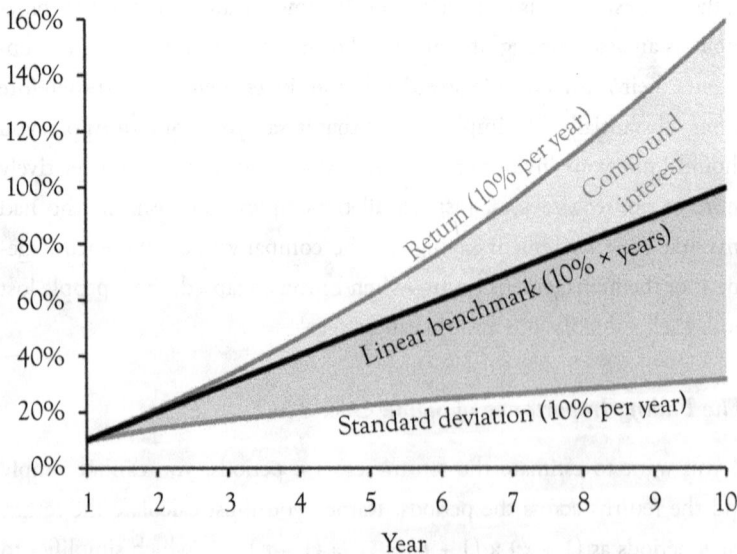

Figure 2.15 Return and standard deviation over time

increasing rate), the standard deviation of return of 10 percent per year over time (which is increasing at a decreasing rate), and a linear benchmark of 10 percent times the number of years. Notice that the expected returns become exponentially *more* important over time, whereas the standard deviation becomes *less* important over time. The implication is that *the longer the investment horizon, the riskier your investment should be.*

Let us explore this implication a bit further with some actual numbers. Suppose that we can invest $100 in either of the following two investments:

a. A low-risk investment with an expected return of 4 percent and an annual standard deviation of 3 percent.
b. A high-risk investment with an expected return of 10 percent and an annual standard deviation of 15 percent.

I simulated what the investment might be worth after 1 through 16 years. Based on the simulations, I made 90 percent confidence intervals, which you can see in Figure 2.16. Thus, you can think of the lower and upper edges of the solid and striped areas as the worst-case and best-case scenarios.

After one year, the low-risk investment might drop to about $99 in the worst case and increase to $109 in the best case, while the high-risk investment might drop to $86 in the worst case or increase to $135 in

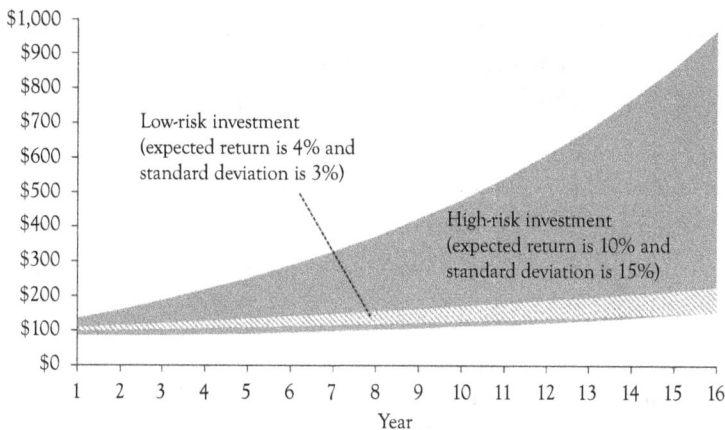

Figure 2.16 Simulated returns for low- and high-risk investments

the best case. Thus, it is not obvious which is the better investment over only one year. Risk-averse investors would probably pick the low-risk investment because of the higher value for the worst-case scenario, while risk-tolerant investors would probably pick the high-risk investment because of the higher expected value.[5]

The magic happens over longer periods. After 16 years, the best-case scenario is naturally much better for the high-risk investment (at $968) than for the low-risk investment (at $225). Now for the magic: the low-risk and high-risk investments have roughly the same worst-case scenarios after 16 years, both with values of roughly $155. What just happened? How can it be that the worst-case scenario for the high-risk investment is no longer worse than the worst-case scenario for the low-risk investment? Crazier yet, if we extrapolate beyond 16 years, the high-risk investment has a better worst-case scenario than the low-risk investment!

There are two reasons for this. The first is that the increase in the standard deviation of returns over time is mercifully modest. This effect plays a more important role for the high-risk investment with the high annual standard deviation and makes it a more appealing investment opportunity for the long run. The second reason is the exponential increase in the expected returns over time, which particularly helps the high-risk investment (with the high expected return per year) in the long run. (This second effect plays an even larger role for the best-case scenarios.)

Let us look at this yet again using historical data for the S&P 500 index and T-bills from the beginning of 1928 to the end of 2020. Suppose that we invested in either the S&P 500 index or T-bills on January 1 of a random year between 1928 and 2000 and hold the investment for exactly one year. Then there would have been a 68 percent chance that the S&P 500 index performed better than the T-bills.[6] This is depicted as the leftmost point in Figure 2.17. Suppose instead that we invested for two years. Then the chance that the S&P 500 index performed better

---

[5] The *expected value* means the *average* across all scenarios.
[6] There are 93 years between 1928 and 2000, and the S&P 500 beat T-bills in 63 in those years, for a fraction of 63/93 = 68%.

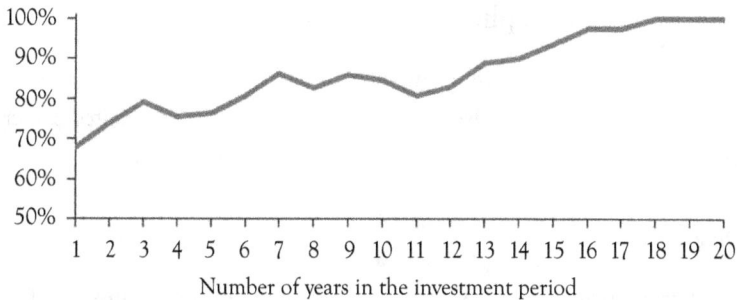

Figure 2.17 Probability that the S&P 500 index outperformed T-bills

than the T-bills would have been 74 percent. Can you guess where this is going? Suppose now that we invested for 18 years. Then the S&P 500 would have been guaranteed to have performed better than the T-bills. The same holds for investment periods longer than 18 years. Thus, there was no investment period of at least 18 years between 1928 and 2020 during which the S&P 500 failed to beat T-bills. That is remarkable, right?[7]

What can we learn from this? While the stock market certainly experiences serious setbacks from time to time, over the longer term, the market recovers sufficiently to beat safer investments. This happens time and time again. I hope this convinces you that *for a longer investment horizon, you should invest in the stock market rather than in safer securities*; you are almost guaranteed to do better, and most likely a lot better.

The examples illustrate that you can disregard the fable about the tortoise and the hare when investing for the long run, meaning at least 15 to 20 years. In that case, slow and steady fails to win every time. The effect from compounding returns has received much of the credit for this, but I think the behavior of standard deviation over time deserves at least as much credit. Anyway, let us not quibble about who deserves more credit; let us just enjoy the magic embedded in long-run investment returns.

---

[7] A caveat is in order. Some might argue that there is a lot of overlap in these long series, and that there are only a few truly independent series, for example, less than five independent series of 20 years each. They might further argue that there would be more extreme observations had we looked at more years of data, and that the next 100 years could encounter more extreme events than the last 100 years. That is certainly possible and might warrant us taking less portfolio risk.

Some Implications for Portfolio Choice

This subsection discusses three implications for investors' portfolio choices. At the risk of being repetitive, the first two implications were stated earlier, so I will be brief. The third implication requires more discussion.

Diversification

Recall from earlier that the standard deviation of returns diminishes when we combine individual securities into a portfolio of securities. The diminishing effect is most pronounced when the individual securities have low correlation, for example, because they come from different sectors like steel and tech. Furthermore, the effect is most pronounced for the first securities that are added to the portfolio and tapers off once the portfolio contains many securities, as shown in Figure 2.18. Once the portfolio consists of some 20 to 30 very different securities, the incremental benefit on total portfolio risk from adding more securities is minimal, and we have a *diversified portfolio*. The risk that we got rid of is called *diversifiable risk* (also called firm-specific or idiosyncratic risk), and it is attributable to risk factors that affect only one or a small set of companies, like the failure of a product launch. The remaining risk is called *systematic risk* (or market risk), and it is caused by broad economic factors, like a change in the interest rate. Fortunately, most stocks contain more diversifiable risk than systematic risk, such that diversification is very effective in reducing risk.

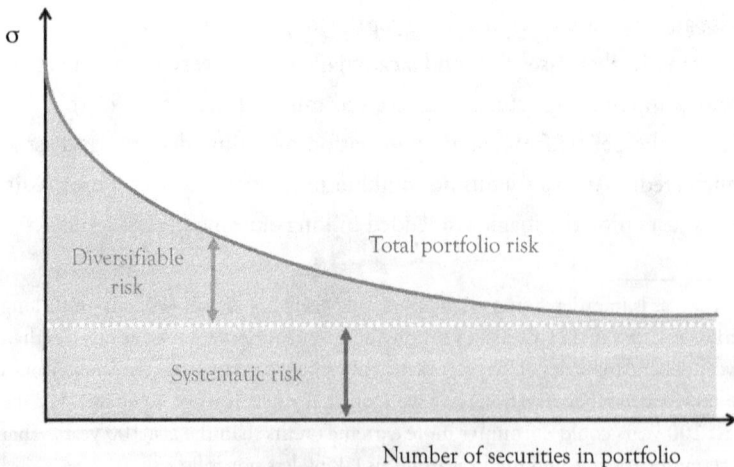

Figure 2.18 The effect of diversification on risk

The implication is that *we should diversify across enough securities in enough sectors that we are only left with systematic risk*. Indeed, finance theory suggests that investors are compensated for holding systematic risk but not for holding diversifiable risk, so there is little reason for risk-averse investors to hold diversifiable risk.[8] That further means that the positive relation that we observed earlier between the average return and the volatility of return holds for diversified portfolios but not necessarily for individual securities.

Investment Horizon and Risk

An earlier subsection explored how the expected return and the volatility of return behave over time. While the expected return grows exponentially with the investment horizon, the volatility of return increases at a more modest pace with the investment horizon. The implication stated earlier is that *we should increase the investment risk with the length of the investment horizon*.

A caveat to this implication is that it primarily pertains to diversified portfolios. That way, the higher risk is accompanied by a higher expected return. Thus, a modified and improved version of the implication is that we should invest in diversified portfolios with low risk when the investment horizon is short and in diversified portfolios with high risk when the investment horizon is long.

An unrelated reason for taking more risk with longer investment horizons is that if the investment performs poorly in the short term, you have sufficient time to change your behavior to get back on track again. For example, if you plan to retire in 20 years, but after the next 10 years your portfolio has performed much worse than expected, you can reduce your living expenses (including expenses at restaurants and vacations), work some overtime, or delay retirement to make up for the lackluster investment performance.

Achieving the Desired Risk Level

Let us return to the earlier example where I plotted the expected returns and standard deviation of returns for three securities (A, B, and C) and combinations of those three securities. I have replicated that plot in

---

[8] An exception would be that you possess favorable inside information about a security. But few of us have such information, and you must be careful not to trade based on inside information because it could be construed as illegal insider trading.

Figure 2.19, except that I highlighted portfolios that are along the *efficient frontier*. For any given expected return that is feasible by combining the three securities, the portfolios along the efficient frontier have the lowest standard deviation. Thus, these represent the best possible portfolio choices for any investor who can only choose from the three securities.

Next, I will extend this by using actual data for many large companies in the United States, including Amazon, Apple, Boeing, Caterpillar, Citigroup, Coca-Cola, Disney, Ford, and JPMorgan Chase. The graph shows the expected return and standard deviation for these individual companies as individual markers, and the efficient frontier based on combinations of these companies is given as a curved line. In addition, I have included a risk-free security with zero standard deviation and a small expected return.[9]

When we combine the risk-free security with a risky security (or a portfolio of risky securities), we end up with a standard deviation that equals the fraction in the risky security multiplied by the standard deviation of the risky security. This is a special case of our earlier discussion, and you will just have to trust me on this one so we can minimize the math in this book. That also means that combinations of the risk-free

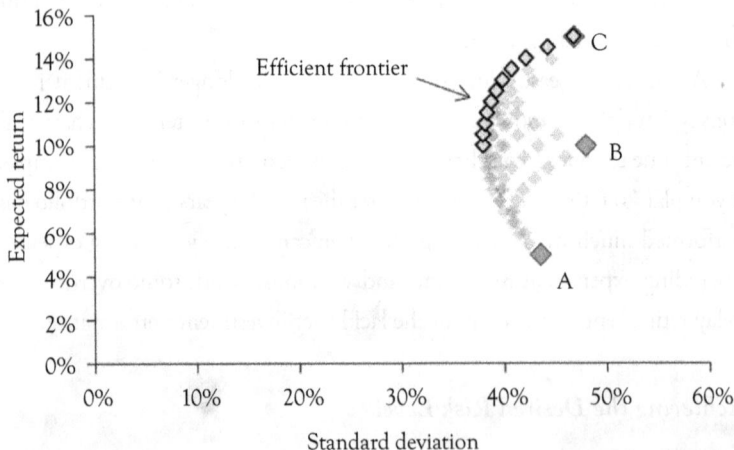

Figure 2.19 The efficient frontier for three securities

---

[9] Yes, I know that we saw earlier that Treasury securities, which are generally viewed to be risk-free, have a standard deviation of a couple of percent. But if we were to match our investment horizon with the maturity of the Treasury security, we could eliminate that risk. Anyway, we will just assume here that the risk-free security has no risk at all.

security and a risky security (or a risky portfolio) in the graph can be represented as a straight line. In Figure 2.20, I could have drawn straight lines between the risk-free security and any of the stock portfolios or individual stocks. But I chose to only draw a straight dashed line between the risk-free security and the portfolio on the efficient frontier that gives the steepest slope. Why is the slope important? The maximum slope means that we get the largest increase in expected return as we increase the risk, that is, we get the greatest bang for the buck.

It turns out that the dashed line is tangent to the efficient frontier where the value-weighted stock market portfolio is located. It is tricky to prove this, and I am not even going to try to do so here. You just have to believe me again. This result turns out to be a big deal. You can see that the points along the dashed line dominate even the efficient frontier, which means that the portfolios along the dashed line represent the best investments available in the graph. Thus, *we should all invest in a combination of the risk-free security and the market portfolio.*

What does this mean in practice? You can simply invest in an index fund that tracks the market and place the rest in risk-free government securities. If you have a long investment horizon (or a high-risk tolerance), you should invest 100 percent in index funds. As your investment horizon gets shorter, you should move money from the index fund to the risk-free security.[10]

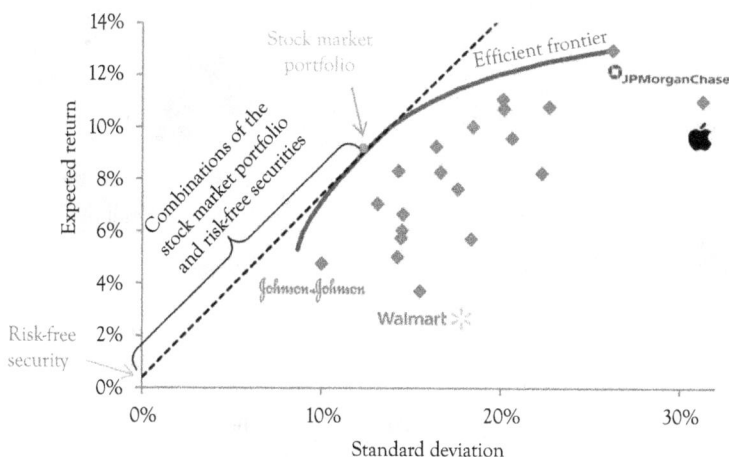

Figure 2.20 Optimal portfolio choices

---

[10] If you want even more risk than what 100 percent in the market index fund can offer, you could borrow to invest more than you have, provided that you can

Where do other investments fit in? If we constrain our discussion for now to liquid securities that trade at U.S. stock exchanges, we should at least mention corporate bonds, REITs (real estate investment trusts, which hold apartments, offices, and other commercial buildings), and foreign stocks.[11] All three of these categories come prepackaged as ETFs, and many individual foreign stocks even trade at U.S. stock exchanges. A further commonality is that they can be used to diversity a portfolio further, thus reducing overall portfolio risk. But they differ in terms of their risk by themselves and correlations with the U.S. stock market; corporate bonds typically have low risk and low correlation with the U.S. stock market, while REITs and stocks from other developed countries typically have high risk and high correlation with the U.S. stock market. I would recommend that individuals invest in REITs and foreign stocks for their diversification benefits and in corporate bonds (and Treasury bonds) primarily to dial back risk as the investment horizon gets shorter. Figure 2.21 displays reasonable allocations of security holdings for two generic investment horizons (with references to ticker symbols of possible Vanguard ETFs in parentheses).

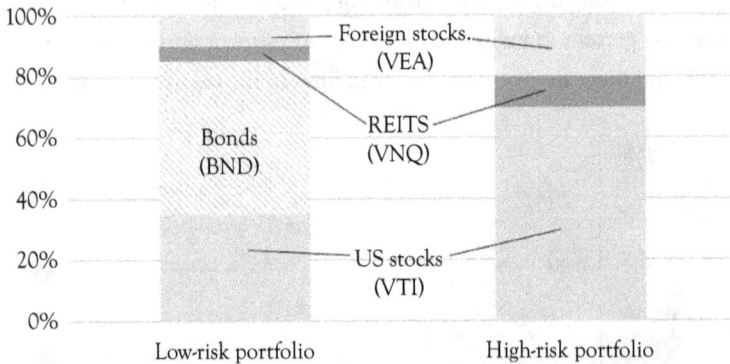

Figure 2.21 *Reasonable allocations of security holdings*

---

borrow cheaply. For example, you might take out a mortgage on the equity in your house and invest that money in the index fund as well. If the mortgage rate is close to the risk-free rate, you effectively move up the dashed line in the graph beyond the location of the stock market portfolio.

[11] I will discuss investments in various insurance products and homes (i.e., houses and condominiums) in a later section because of their added complexities and unique financing.

CHAPTER 3

Market Efficiency and Investment Psychology

The concept of market efficiency is critical for financial markets, and the degree to which financial markets are efficient has important implications for individual investors' optimal choices. Furthermore, investors often behave irrationally, so it is helpful to recognize and avoid behavioral traps that hurt investment performance.

The main objectives for this chapter are:

- Develop an understanding of:
  - o Market efficiency; and
  - o Why market efficiency implies that individual investors should shun active investment management.
- Learn common behavioral traps that hurt investment performance.

Market Efficiency and the Performance of Passive Versus Active Management

Every stock has a true value that depends on the prospects and risks of the company. Of course, no one can predict the prospects with certainty, and different investors make different predictions that result in different valuations. The stock price, therefore, reflects the average, or consensus, of all those predictions and valuations.

The question then is: How close is the stock price to the true value? If investors have access to all relevant information about the prospects and the risks of the company, and they use that information properly when making predictions and estimating values, the stock price should come close to the true value. That brings us to the notion of market efficiency.

Market efficiency means that stock prices reflect all available, relevant information. (*Semistrong efficiency* narrows this down to *public* information.) That does not quite mean that stock prices are identical to the true value, but rather that the deviations are random and that stock prices adjust quickly to the arrival of new information. Thus, no one knows whether the current stock prices are too low or too high.

What if only a few investors have access to some highly relevant information? If those investors are either (i) dominant, like large hedge funds, or (ii) corporate insiders, who have special access to information and whose trades are closely monitored, *and* they use that information to trade the stock, the stock price should adjust to reflect the information. Otherwise, the stock price would not reflect the information. For example, if a corporate insider possesses unique information about a new product launch, that information would not be reflected in the stock price until the insider starts trading on it, and other investors can observe that trading.

It is reasonable to assume that stock prices reflect much of the relevant information but not all. The next question then is: Is it worthwhile for investors to seek out and analyze the information that is not reflected? That depends on many factors:

- How much information is not reflected in the stock price? Unfortunately, we will never know this.
- How difficult and expensive is it to find that information? Some of it might be hidden inside the company, some might be circulating among suppliers and customers, and some might be in plain sight, like in a footnote of the financial statements.
- What is the source of the information? If the information comes from corporate insiders, trading on it might be illegal.
- Can investors determine whether the information they discover is already reflected in the stock price (assuming that it is not insider information), and, if so, how it should affect the stock price? This entails a careful and precise valuation based on all public information, including what the investors discover.

- How much money do the investors have to invest? Taking advantage of a small mispricing generally requires substantial investments to make it worthwhile.

It quickly becomes apparent that it is generally worthless for individual investors to seek out and analyze information that might affect stock prices. They simply lack the necessary network, skills, and resources. It might not even be worthwhile for most professional traders with expertise and resources to do so. If it were, we should observe that professional traders who actively seek out undervalued stocks perform better than other investors.

How well do professional money managers perform then? There is plenty of research on the performance of actively managed funds, but it is a controversial field because there are many parties with vested interests, especially the actively managed funds themselves. In short, the bulk of the reliable evidence suggests that, on average, actively managed funds fail to beat passive funds with similar risk. For example, S&P SPIVA reports that 75 percent of large-cap funds underperformed the S&P 500 (using data up to the end of 2020). Furthermore, there is little evidence that funds that have performed well in the past perform better than other funds in subsequent periods, suggesting that their past performance was primarily due to luck (which is temporary) rather than skill (which is more permanent).[1]

---

[1] Bill Sharpe, the winner of the 1990 Nobel Memorial Prize in Economics, put forth a simple arithmetic argument for why active investors struggle in their pursuit of superior performance. Suppose that there are only two types of investors: (1) those who invest in index funds that passively hold identical portions in all publicly traded companies and (2) hedge funds and other large institutional investors that are actively managed, meaning that they spend resources to identify undervalued stocks in which to invest. The index funds, owning, say 20 percent of each firm, will necessarily earn the average return of the market. If so, the hedge funds as a group (owning 80 percent of each firm), will necessarily also earn the average return of the market. The only way that a given hedge fund can earn a superior return is if (a) some other hedge funds earn an inferior return or (b) we introduce other types of investors, like day traders, who earn an inferior return.

To be fair, the aforementioned evidence does not preclude the possibility that fund managers can identify undervalued stocks. Rather, it means that any such skills do not seem to benefit the investors in actively managed funds. There are several possible reasons for this. First, the actively managed funds spend substantial resources on identifying suitable trades, and these costs, and perhaps more, are paid by the investors in the funds. For example, a common fee structure for hedge funds is 2 percent of the value invested and 20 percent of the profits, which is quite steep. Second, active trading contributes to substantial costs that might be incorporated into the stock prices that are paid or received. Third, there is plenty of anecdotal evidence that managers at actively managed funds keep the best trades for their personal portfolios.

In 2008, Warren Buffett, the oracle of Omaha, made the point that actively managed funds underperform when he challenged the hedge fund industry to a bet that a passive index fund strategy would outperform actively managed hedge funds. Buffett was confident that he would win because the hedge funds are burdened with large costs. Protégé Partners LLC accepted a bet of a million dollars. Buffett easily won the bet; his pick, the Vanguard's S&P 500 Admiral fund (VFIAX) gained 126 percent, whereas the five hedge funds picked by Protégé Partners added an average of 36 percent. While this is just anecdotal evidence, it suggests that it is hard for active fund managers to outperform the market when considering the costs of such efforts.

Market efficiency also implies that the stock market is forgiving to those who are uninformed. Even if you know nothing about the stocks you trade or how to assess their value, you get the same fair price as everyone else. That is certainly not the case in all markets. For example, if you get into the market for art or vintage cars, you better know what you are doing and how to value the assets to avoid being duped.

Where does this leave us? I would argue that investing in actively managed funds is foolish, though you will no doubt find cases where it has paid off, just like the lottery has paid off for some. Investing in broad index funds certainly seems a lot more sensible. What about investing in individual stocks? If we cannot tell which stocks are priced too high and which are priced too low, it seems like we should all be able to

Figure 3.1 Stock picking with darts

choose stocks by throwing darts on pages with stock ticker symbols, as in Figure 3.1. This is actually quite close. But if you use a random process to compose your stock portfolio, you should also ensure that the portfolio is sufficiently diversified across many sectors and that it has the desired level of risk and expected return. So, you might have to rethrow some darts if too many end up in certain sectors. And, if the resulting portfolio is too risky, you could dial down the risk by investing a larger proportion of your wealth in low-risk fixed income securities.

Investment Psychology and Behavioral Traps

Market efficiency presumes that investors are rational. However, research in psychology and finance has documented that individual investors (and noninvestors, for that matter) can be quite irrational. Such irrationality could be a reason for markets to be inefficient. More importantly for the readers of this book, irrational investor behavior can be detrimental to individual investors' wealth. Thus, it is worthwhile to discuss some of the behavioral traps that investors should recognize and avoid.

Overconfidence

Individuals tend to be overconfident about their own abilities and prospects. (For the male readers out there: this particularly pertains to you!) For example, some 80 percent of us claim to be better than average at driving a car. Such confidence and optimism can be helpful in many aspects of our lives but not necessarily when investing for at least two reasons.

First, research shows that overconfidence causes more frequent trading. And here is the bad news for frequent traders: frequent trading is associated with worse performance, at least partially because of higher trading costs.[2] In addition, frequent trading results in higher taxation for reasons discussed in the chapter on tax strategies, the most important of which is that trading triggers capital gain realizations.[3] The harmful effect of frequent trading is especially relevant for day traders (as illustrated in Figure 3.2), who buy and sell securities throughout the day under the illusion that they can successfully time the market.

Figure 3.2 Day trader

---

[2] While brokerage commissions have been driven down to zero in recent years, there are other less apparent trading costs, including the bid-ask spread, that is, the difference between the prices when you sell versus buy a security.

[3] OK, clever readers will realize later that they can curtail this adverse tax effect by restricting the frequent trading to tax-favored accounts with a large menu of investment choices, for example, IRAs. I even make a note of that in a later chapter.

Second, overconfidence is likely to lead to excessive risk, both systematic and diversifiable risk. I will advocate for taking substantial investment risk in this book for long-term investment horizons, and likely more than most individuals are comfortable with initially. However, I will only advocate for *systematic* risk because it is accompanied by higher expected return, and not *diversifiable* risk, which can be removed via diversification and does not come with higher return. Furthermore, there is a limit to how much risk (even systematic risk) is appropriate, and there are times when we should dial down the risk, especially as we approach retirement and beyond.

Herding and FOMO

Individuals naturally socialize and interact with each other, and those interactions affect our opinions and behavior. Thus, if a friend recommends a stock, you are more likely to buy it. And if those around us start selling, we might follow, like a flock of startled pigeons that lack independent thinking, as in Figure 3.3.

In the age of the Internet and social media, FOMO has been recognized as a driver of collective behavior and herding. In general, FOMO refers to the fear of missing out on the fun and experiences that others have. In the investment world, FOMO refers to the fear of missing out on

Figure 3.3 Flock of startled pigeons

promising opportunities. It is annoying to hear of other investors striking gold by investing in, say, Bitcoin, GameStop, or Tesla. We simply become envious and greedy. Thus, we might be enticed to get in on the same stocks or whatever is pitched as the next hot investment.

Investor herding comes with several drawbacks:

- You become more vulnerable to various schemes that depend on investor herding, including pump and dump schemes, where scammers hype stocks to temporarily inflate the price, and pyramid schemes, where new investors are attracted by false promises of high payoffs.
- You might end up trading too frequently and taking excessive risk, thus having the same problems as the overconfident investors discussed earlier.
- You might end up with a portfolio that has excessive exposure to the local economy because your friends hype local firms or certain sectors (see further discussion in the familiarity bias section next).

Familiarity Bias

When investors buy individual securities, they gravitate toward companies that they know, including those that they work for, are located nearby, produce products that the investors use, or have recognizable brand names. It is no surprise that GameStop and AMC Entertainment—familiar names among gamers and retail investors who participate in online forums—became so-called meme stocks during the pandemic rather than obscure companies in the chemicals or materials sectors.

To the extent that familiarity gives investors an informational advantage when valuing stocks, investing in familiar stocks might produce superior returns. Unfortunately, investors overrate their informational advantage relative to professional investors, such that familiarity fails to produce superior returns. Instead, familiarity bias breeds poorly diversified portfolios, for example, portfolios that are too heavy on tech and retail stocks or companies close to investors' homes (often referred to as *home bias*).

In this context, we should be particularly aware of the role of our labor capital. Our current and future income represents an important source of future wealth accumulation. Some people can easily find alternative employment with similar pay if their employer struggles, while others would suffer financially if their employer must dismiss them or cut their pay. The latter group is financially dependent on their employer and, thus, should refrain from investing their savings in that company, irrespective of how well they believe they know the company. They should rather invest in geographically distant companies that operate in unrelated sectors. Take a lesson from the rank-and-file employees of Enron who mistakenly believed the company to be in solid shape and kept most of their retirement funds invested in the company until it sank, as illustrated in Figure 3.4. (Yes, I know that I mentioned the Enron case before, but it is a lesson worth repeating.)

Figure 3.4 Enron employees

Extrapolation Bias

We all learn from past experiences and observations, and we use that knowledge when projecting the future. This is generally beneficial. For example, touching a hot stove top teaches us a helpful lesson to be more careful the next time.

In the finance arena, we use past securities returns to extrapolate into the future. Thus, if a security has delivered poor returns in the past, we project that security to also deliver poor returns in the future, and vice versa for a security that has delivered strong returns in the past. If we use a long history of returns, these extrapolations are reasonable. For example, in an earlier section, we used historical returns for Treasury securities and stocks during the last 90 years to show that the latter group has performed significantly better, and we can therefore expect stocks to also outperform Treasury securities in the future.

The problem is that we tend to overemphasize the most recent returns when projecting the future. Consider the two graphs in Figure 3.5 that I made using the same random number generator, and, therefore, should have the same returns if I were to extend the series. The arrows show what many investors would extrapolate future returns to be based on the most recent returns. Because the most recent returns for the graph on the right are stronger than those on the left by pure chance, investors also expect future returns to be stronger. This incorrect inference is called *extrapolation bias*.

Extrapolation bias can be treacherous for investors:

- Extrapolation bias causes investors to buy stocks after recent market run-ups and chase stocks, sectors, and funds with a strong recent performance. This clashes with the steady and disciplined savings behavior that produces strong portfolios in the long run. Furthermore, it might result in a poorly diversified portfolio concentrating on sectors that happen to have had the strongest recent performance.

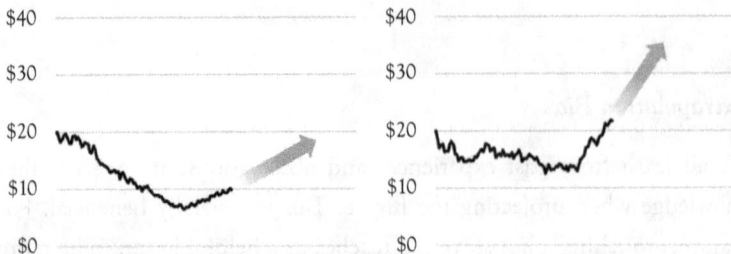

Figure 3.5 Extrapolation of returns

- Extrapolation bias causes investors to be overly optimistic about the future following recent market run-ups, thus making many to mistakenly believe that their portfolios will grow to be sufficient for their retirement years.

Framing and Pension Decisions

Individuals are affected by the framing of questions and decisions. For example, people generally estimate $2 \times 3 \times 4 \times 5 \times 6 \times 7 \times 8$ to be less than $8 \times 7 \times 6 \times 5 \times 4 \times 3 \times 2$ unless they compare them directly and recognize that they must, of course, be the same. Or you might view a yoghurt that is "90% fat-free" to be healthier than one that contains "10% fat."

Individuals also look at the range of prices and product characteristics for guidance of what is reasonable, which, in turn, affects their choices. Thus, if presented with two wine bottles at a restaurant at $30 and $40, respectively, they might consider the $40 wine too expensive. But if presented with a third bottle at $60, they might consider the $40 wine to be reasonably priced. Marketers exploit this tendency by presenting products with high prices in the product line-up as decoys to make us purchase a higher-priced product. The wine example also has another behavioral framing twist, which is that individuals tend to choose the second cheapest wine on the menu over the cheapest one so as not to look cheap.

The makers of the payment systems for coffee shops and similar retailers use framing to increase tips. You might purchase a cappuccino and a muffin at a local coffee shop and be presented with the touch screen choices as shown in Figure 3.6.[4] Before these payment systems arrived, most individuals would not tip much in such cases. But the screen encourages a sizable tip for three reasons: (i) customers are led to believe that a tip of at least 15 percent is reasonable, (ii) customers might miss the subtle choices below the bold choices of 15, 20, and 25 percent, and (iii) customers avoid "custom tip amount" and "no tip"

---

[4] For purchases below $10, the default of the payment system might be to suggest tips of one, two, or three dollars instead.

Figure 3.6 Tipping menu

because those choices would make them look cheap to the barista and others in line.

The framing effect has been shown to be particularly consequential when individuals make pension decisions:

- Individuals sometimes elect whether to participate in a retirement plan. Whether they participate often depends on whether they have to opt-in or opt-out, that is, whether the default is not to participate or to participate if they fail to act. In particular, the participation rate turns out to be much greater if the default is to participate. In this case, the default option is likely viewed as the recommended option that less knowledgeable employees happily follow. (Of course, it might also be that some individuals are just being inattentive or too lazy to make a choice.)
- If individuals are presented with investment options (e.g., mutual funds) with varying risk, people choose more of what they perceive to be moderate, which they infer to be the middle ones. The implication is that the inclusion of more high-risk mutual funds in the menu of choices induces employees to take more risk with their retirement funds.

- Some individuals pursue a naïve diversification of investing equally in all investment choices on the menu. Thus, they will choose relatively more stocks with three stock funds and one bond fund on the menu than with one stock fund and three bond funds on the menu.
- Some individuals are overwhelmed with too many investment choices on the menu, causing them to delay making decisions, sometimes indefinitely.

If you find yourself helplessly lost in these types of situations, I advise you to always participate in whatever retirement funds you can and invest in portfolios that resemble what I presented at the end of the prior chapter. And try to minimize the fees, as I mention several times in this book.

Lack of Self-Control

We all lack self-control at times. I cannot help myself if I see an open chocolate bar on the kitchen counter—my desire always defeats my willpower at that moment. To overcome my moments of weakness, I do not buy much chocolate in the first place, and I will not leave chocolate out as a visible temptation.

Our society is filled with tempting services and material goods, most of which we really do not need. But if we have easy access to money, there is a good chance that we splurge, especially in the early life stages. Think teenagers.

Thus, we need to impose some financial discipline in our lives. Perhaps the best discipline is to have our employer regularly deduct money from our paycheck to be placed in a retirement account. That way, there is a bit of a barrier between you and your funds, as illustrated in Figure 3.7. Beyond the psychological barrier of the money being in an account earmarked for retirement, there is often a financial penalty if you withdraw money from that account too early. The added benefit of contributing to a retirement account is the tax advantage, which we cover later.

Figure 3.7 Barrier to savings

The Disposition Effect and What to Sell

Investors generally exhibit a *disposition effect*, meaning that they are inclined to sell winning stocks and to hold on to losing ones. Perhaps the inclination to sell winning stocks arises from the joy and pride of realizing profits. And perhaps the reluctance to sell losing stocks arises from the pain of realizing losses. Regardless, such behavior is generally harmful for investors' tax burden. It is typically better to realize capital losses early and defer capital gains to the future, as a later chapter will embellish.

CHAPTER 4

Tax Strategies

Taxes can drain substantial value from individuals' wealth. However, the tax code allows investors substantial flexibility and even loopholes to limit the tax drain.

The main objectives for this chapter are:

- Develop a basic understanding of taxation of income from employment and investments.
- Learn to minimize the tax burden by:
  o Using tax-favored accounts; and
  o Exploiting an array of tactics to defer and eliminate capital gains in regular brokerage accounts.

What Is Taxed?

Figure 4.1 illustrates the taxes we pay to the government. But the tax code is complicated with a myriad of tax rates, qualifiers, and exemptions. Let us start with the basic tax rates on income from employment and investments.

Taxes on Employment Income

Figure 4.2 shows the federal marginal tax rate on employment income for single filers and married couples filing jointly for 2023. The tax rate is progressive, meaning that it increases with income level. For example, for an individual filing income of $50,000, the marginal tax rate is 22 percent (meaning that the next dollar of income would be taxed at 22 percent) and the average tax rate is (10% × $11,000 + 12% × ($44,725 − $11,000) + 22% × (50,000 − $44,725))/$50,000 = 12.6%. If the income increases

Figure 4.1 Taxes

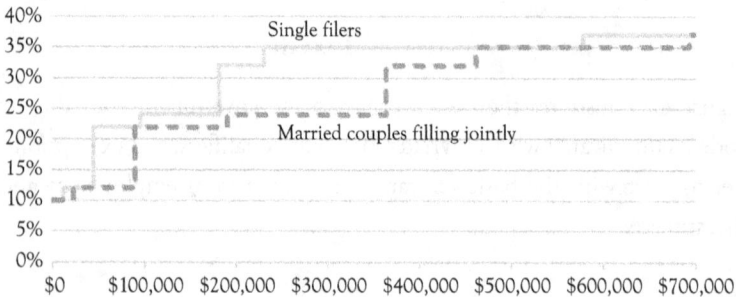

Figure 4.2 Marginal tax rates on employment income

to $250,000, the marginal tax rate is 35 percent and the average tax rate is 25.7 percent.

The figure is a bit deceptive in that it does not capture deductions. For example, the standard deduction for individual filers for 2023 is $13,850, meaning that individual filers do not pay any taxes until they make at least $13,850.

In addition, most states tax income at various rates up to 12.3 percent (for high-income individuals in California). A typical taxpayer with income of $100,000 will therefore face a marginal tax rate on income of 25 to 30 percent.

Taxes on Investment Income

Most interest income (e.g., from fixed-income securities) is taxed as employment income. However, interest from Treasury bonds is exempt from state income taxes, while interest from municipal bonds is exempt from federal income taxes and often from state income taxes, especially when the bonds are issued in the investor's home state. Although zero-coupon bonds pay no interest, a pro-rated portion must be reported as interest for tax purposes each year.

Taxes on dividends depend on the income level and whether the dividends are deemed to be *qualified*. Generally, dividends are deemed to be qualified if the firms paying them are domestic and the investor has held the stock for more than 60 days. Qualified dividends are taxed at the favored tax rate shown in Figure 4.3. Nonqualified dividends are taxed as ordinary employment income, which implies a higher tax rate. Dividends of foreign stock can also be subject to additional foreign taxes, but this is eligible for a Foreign Tax Credit.

Taxes on capital gains occur upon the sale of the securities, that is, when the capital gains are realized, and depend on whether the securities have been held for more than one year, in which case they are deemed

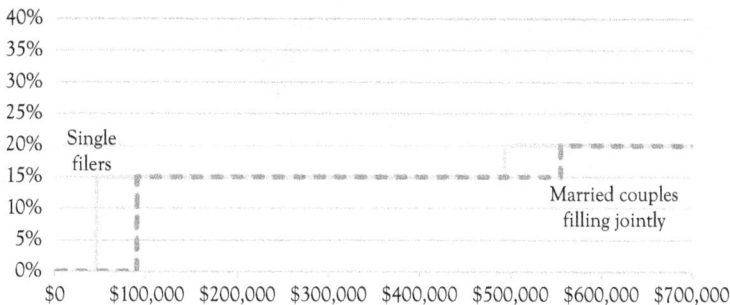

Figure 4.3 Marginal tax rates on favored investment income

to be long-term. Realized long-term capital gains are taxed at the same favored tax rate as qualified dividends. Realized short-term capital gains are taxed at the employment tax rate.[1]

If an investor has sold some securities for a capital gain and others for a capital loss in a year, the taxable capital gain is the net of the realized gains and losses. For this netting calculation, the long-term and short-term capital gains/losses are kept separate. If the realized losses (either long-term or short-term) exceed the realized gains, the investor can claim up to $3,000 of the net losses against ordinary income. The remaining net losses can be carried forward to future years.[2]

Table 4.1 summarizes the tax rates for various categories of investment income. Furthermore, investors with a high income ($200K for

Table 4.1 Tax rates for various types of investment income

	Interest income	Dividends	Capital gains
Favored tax rate		Qualified dividends	Realized long-term capital gains
Employment income tax rate	Most interest income (with possible exceptions for Treasury and municipal bonds)	Nonqualified dividends	Realized short-term capital gains

---

[1] Municipal bonds that are purchased at a discount trigger capital gains taxation upon redemption, and the *de minimis tax rule* states that the tax rate depends on the magnitude of the discount. For small discounts (*de minimis* in tax-speak), defined as less than 0.25 percent for each full year from the purchase date to maturity, the capital gain is taxed at the capital gains tax rate; for large discounts, the capital gain is taxed as ordinary income. Thus, beware of purchasing municipal bonds after interest rates have risen and bond prices have fallen.

[2] You can follow four steps for this. First, you calculate the net short-term capital gain (or loss) and the net long-term capital gain (or loss) separately. Second, you net the long-term gain (or loss) against the short-term gain (or loss). Third, you can use any remaining net capital loss (whether short-term or long-term) to reduce ordinary income up to $3,000. Fourth, you treat the remainders after the prior steps as follows: the net short-term gain is taxed at the ordinary income tax rate, the net long-term gain is taxed at the favorable investment income tax rate, the net short-term loss can be carried over indefinitely and retains its short-term classification, and the net long-term loss can be carried over indefinitely and retains its long-term classification.

single filers and $250K for married couples filing jointly) must pay an additional 3.8 percent net investment income tax (NIIT) on investment income. Most states also charge additional taxes on investment income, and it is often the same rate as for employment income.

Based on the table, it appears that interest income is taxed the most on average, while dividends and capital gains are taxed similarly (assuming that the distribution of dividends across qualified and nonqualified is similar to the distribution of capital gains across long-term and short-term). However, capital gains are effectively taxed less than other investment income because, as noted earlier, capital gains are only taxed when realized, meaning that the taxes are deferred until the securities are sold. Deferring taxes is valuable because the deferred taxes generate investment income while it is deferred. Investors can even exploit the ability to net out capital gains and losses in a given year to defer capital gains taxes further. And in some cases, the deferred tax liability evaporates upon death. We will get back to strategies to defer, and possibly eliminate, capital gains taxes in a later subsection.

Taxes on Investment Income From Foreign Securities

Investing in foreign securities can enhance diversification benefits but also adds some tax complications. The bad news is that even if you are based in the United States, foreign governments are likely to tax dividends and interest, and perhaps even capital gains. The good news is that the U.S. tax code offers a so-called *foreign tax credit* for taxes paid abroad to avoid double taxation.

Suppose that a foreign government has withheld $1,500 as taxes on your foreign investment income, so you get a $1,500 foreign tax credit. What happens next depends on whether the tax on the same investment under the U.S. tax code is above or below what was withheld abroad:

- Suppose that under the U.S. tax code, the tax on the same investment income is $1,700. In that case, you can use the $1,500 foreign tax credit to reduce your U.S. tax bill to $200.

- Suppose that under the U.S. tax code, the tax on the same investment income is $1,200. In that case, you can use $1,200 of the foreign tax credit to reduce your U.S. tax bill to $0 and carry forward the remaining $300 foreign tax credit up to 10 years.

In essence, you end up paying the maximum of what the tax is under the foreign and U.S. tax codes.

Account Types

Regular (Nontax-Favored) Brokerage Accounts

You can quickly and easily open a personal brokerage account with, say, Fidelity or Charles Schwab. Then you can transfer money from, for example, your bank accounts and start investing and trading in a universe of stocks and other securities. At the end of the calendar year, the brokerage firm supplies a summary of investment income, including interest, dividends, and realized short-term and long-term capital gains/losses, which you must report to the Internal Revenue Service (IRS) for the purpose of calculating your taxes.

As your investments in your personal brokerage account grow, the associated investment income can trigger substantial tax bills. Thus, as soon you open the account, you should consider strategies that reduce the tax burden in the long run by (i) allocating certain types of investments to your personal brokerage account versus tax-favored accounts and (ii) making strategic trades at the end of the calendar year and potentially other times. I return to these strategies later.

Tax-Favored Accounts

Many investment accounts, including retirement accounts (e.g., 401(k), 403(b), 457(b), IRA, and Roth IRA) and college savings accounts, come with tax advantages. I will discuss these accounts in greater detail later. For now, it is sufficient to emphasize that the accounts essentially allow the investments to grow tax-free, meaning that there is no tax on the investment income. In some cases, employment income can be deposited into the accounts before taxes are paid, and employment taxes are paid once the funds are withdrawn from the account. In other cases, after-tax funds can be deposited into the accounts, and no further taxes are paid on the funds while it stays in the account, nor when the funds are withdrawn from the account. If the employment tax rate is the same at the times of deposit and withdrawal, I show later that the two types of tax-favored accounts give identical tax savings.

Asset Location: What Investments to Place in Regular Versus Tax-Favored Accounts

Because tax-favored accounts evade taxes on investment income, we should keep most our financial investments (stocks, bonds, etc.) in such accounts. In fact, this is so important that I will repeat it: *we should keep most of our financial investments in tax-favored accounts!*

However, there are three reasons why individuals must or should place some investments in regular brokerage accounts as well:

- Most importantly, there are constraints to how much we can deposit in tax-favored accounts, so some of our investments might have to spill over to regular brokerage accounts, as Figure 4.4 illustrates.
- The tax-favored accounts often lock up the funds (unless you pay a penalty) for a longer period or until certain conditions are met. Thus, regular accounts generally provide better liquidity.
- We will explore a benefit later from investments in regular brokerage accounts, namely loss harvesting. That benefit suggests that we should maintain a modest regular brokerage account. Admittedly, though, I mostly think of this as an incidental benefit of having a regular brokerage account and not the reason for funding the account.

Given that most individuals end up with both tax-favored and regular brokerage accounts, a relevant question is: What securities should we keep in which account? With some tax-favored accounts, there are

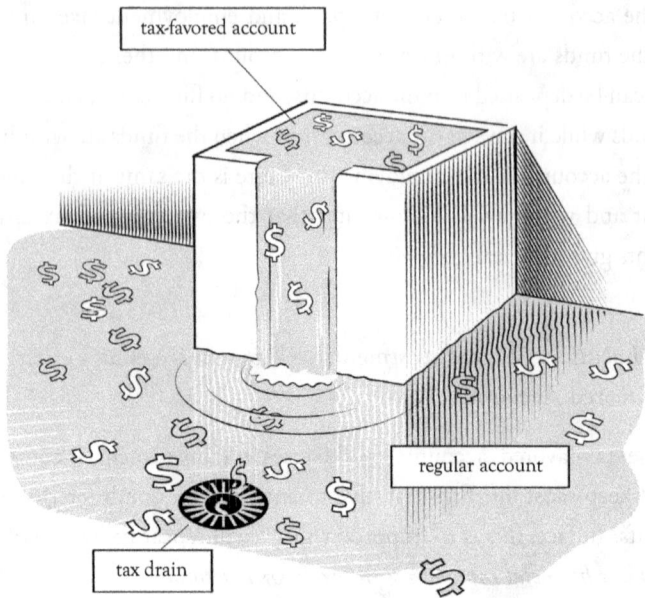

Figure 4.4 *Tax-favored and regular accounts*

some limits to what you can hold, but even then, there is considerable flexibility.

Let me start with two general guidelines:

Guideline #1: *Keep securities with high investment income in the tax-favored accounts.*

The simple reason for this is that the higher the return, the more important the tax exemption. Peter Thiel, a cofounder of PayPal, exploited this when he bought a few thousand dollars' worth of pre-IPO shares in PayPal a couple of decades ago inside a tax-favored account (specifically, a Roth IRA, which we cover later). Because of an exceptionally high return, the investment had grown to five billion dollars by 2021, but Thiel does not have to pay any taxes on this. In fact, he can let it continue to grow tax-free for as long as he wishes. Pretty crazy, eh?

Guideline #2: *Keep securities with investment income that is taxed heavily (including interest income, dividends, and short-term capital gains) in the tax-favored accounts, and securities with investment income that is taxed lightly (including long-term capital gains and tax-exempt interest) in regular accounts.*

This guideline is rooted in the earlier discussion of how different types of investment income are taxed. Recall that interest income is taxed more than dividends, and dividends are taxed more than capital gains. Thus, it generally makes sense to place investments with great interest income, and possibly those with great dividends, in tax-favored accounts and investments with mostly capital gains in regular brokerage accounts.

The two guidelines form the two dimensions in Figure 4.5. Securities with both high investment income and high taxation on that income should definitely go in the tax-favored accounts, whereas securities with low investment income and low taxation on that income can go in regular accounts.

However, there are few categories of securities that are high along both dimensions or low on both dimensions; those that have high investment income tend to have low taxation of that income, and vice versa. You can see this tendency in my rough placement of security categories along the diagonal from the upper left to the lower right in the figure.

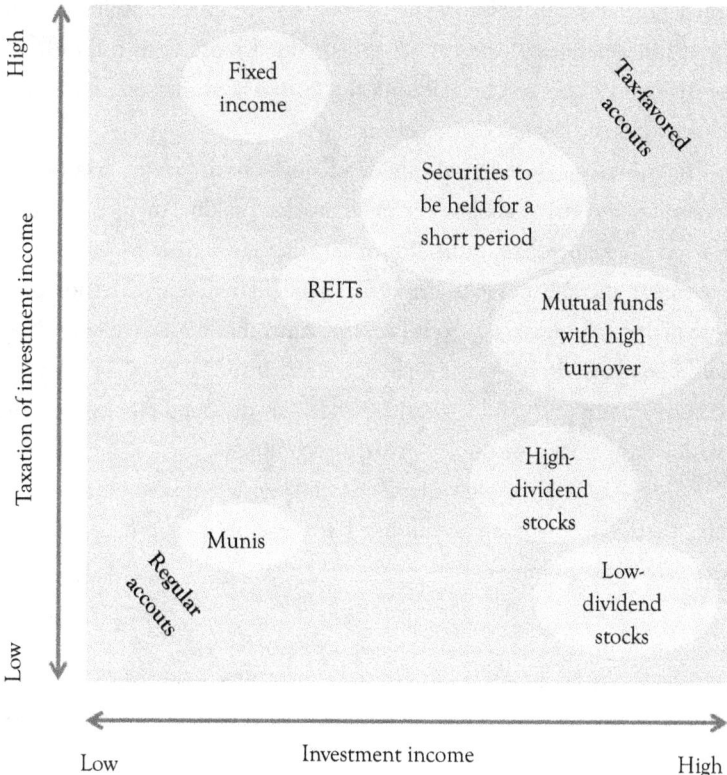

Figure 4.5 Asset location

Let me proceed with more specific advice.[3] But keep in mind the earlier recommendation that if there is capacity in the tax-favored account, we should place most securities there. The subsequent discussion assumes that there is not enough capacity in our tax-favored accounts, so we must resort to regular accounts as well.

Fixed-income securities (i.e., bonds): Fixed-income securities have low to modest interest income and high taxation of that income, making the placement of those securities ambiguous. If the securities are high-yield bonds (sometimes called junk bonds), their investment income is higher, and I would place them in a tax-favored account, whereas if the securities are government bonds, their investment income is low, and I would place them in a regular account.

Low-dividend stocks: Low-dividend stocks have high investment income, but this income comes from capital gains that have low taxation. The next section discusses ways to minimize the tax burden from capital gains, both by deferring them and, in some cases, annulling them. If you can defer/annul the capital gains (which most of us can do), the low-dividend stocks can be placed in the regular accounts, otherwise they should go in the tax-favored accounts.

High-dividend stocks: High-dividend stocks have greater taxation on investment income than low-dividend stocks, making them more suitable for tax-favored accounts. However, they also tend to have lower investment income because firms that pay high dividends tend to be more mature and less risky, so it is not obvious that high-dividend stocks should be placed in the tax-favored accounts. If forced to make a general recommendation, I would prioritize the high-dividend stocks over the low-dividend stocks for the tax-favored accounts.

REITs: REITs have high dividends and modest investment income. Thus, their placement is unclear, but I am leaning toward keeping them in tax-favored accounts.

---

[3] If you seek advice on this issue other places, including web pages of respected financial institutions and financial advisers, you might find different advice. But beware that they tend to focus on only one dimension, the taxation of investment income, and not the magnitude of investment income, which should also be considered.

Municipal bonds (munis): The interest from munis is exempted from federal income taxes and possibly from state income taxes. The tax exemption causes their pretax investment income to be lower. Thus, munis should be kept in regular accounts. In fact, it makes no sense to invest in munis inside tax-favored accounts because you could instead buy regular bonds with higher pretax investment income and, thus, higher post-tax investment income given the tax-favored status of the account; it only makes sense to buy munis if you have a high tax rate on income and no way to shield your interest income from that high income tax rate.

Securities to be held for a short period: If you intend to hold securities for a short period, the frequent realizations of capital gains make it more sensible to hold the securities in a tax-favored account. Thus, if you engage in day trading (which, incidentally, I strongly discourage), you should do so in a tax-favored account. However, there is a counterargument to placing short-term investments in tax-favored accounts. The reason for the short-term investment perspective might be that you anticipate a liquidity need within a short period, for example, to buy a car or a house. If so, I would caution against placing the funds in tax-favored accounts because these accounts are generally designed for long-term investments and often (but not always) come with (i) penalties for early withdrawals and (ii) restrictions in returning the funds to the tax-favored accounts once it is withdrawn, as we will see later.

Mutual funds with high turnover, such as actively managed funds: In the previous section, I advised against holding actively managed mutual funds because of their lackluster performance when accounting for their high fees. But if you insist on holding them, it makes sense to place them in the tax-favored accounts because their relatively high trading activity triggers frequent realizations of capital gains and nonqualified dividends. Thus, even if you simply buy and hold the fund, you might not be able to defer the realization of capital gains or deem dividends as qualified. Index mutual funds with substantial redemptions might suffer from the same problem, though it is much smaller. I discuss this tax inefficiency further in the chapter on funds, along with how ETFs avoid the problem.

Target-date funds: I discuss target-date funds in detail in a later chapter. For now, it is sufficient to know that they are mutual funds with various types of securities that automatically trim their stock positions over time in favor of fixed income. This exchange of securities triggers capital gains, making them better suited for tax-favored accounts.

Foreign securities: I would place foreign securities in the regular accounts for two reasons. First, this is the only way that the foreign tax credit from withheld taxes on these securities can be used; if you place the foreign securities in a tax-favored account, the foreign tax-credit go to waste. Second, foreign securities tend to have greater volatility (at least in U.S. dollar terms) and a smaller correlation with the U.S. market than domestic securities, which increases the chance that they can be used for tax loss harvesting.[4]

How to Minimize Taxes in Regular (Nontax-Favored) Accounts

Now that we have concluded that most of the investment income in the regular accounts should stem from capital gains, we should consider how we can limit the taxation of those capital gains, as Figure 4.6 illustrates.

Figure 4.6 Avoiding taxes

---

[4] The combination of large dividends/interest income associated with many foreign securities and the taxes withheld by foreign governments makes it hard to avoid or defer taxes. Thus, had it not been for their diversification benefits, I would have stayed away from foreign securities.

Extend the Holding Period

There are two reasons for extending the holding period of investments with considerable capital gains. First, if you hold the investments for at least one year, the capital gains change status from "short-term" to "long-term" and enjoy a lower tax rate. Second, the realization of the capital gains, and, hence, the capital gains tax, is deferred so that the deferred tax can continue to generate investment income. We will see later that we might even be able to neutralize those gains. Thus, after buying stocks, you should just sit back and watch their rising value over many years without selling them, as Figure 4.7 illustrates.

Figure 4.7 Enjoying long-term capital gains

Choose the Optimal Tax Lot

If you have bought a stock at different points in time (and, thus, at different prices) and then choose to sell a part of the holdings, you can choose which shares you sell. That is, even though the shares are identical, you can choose the basis price among the various prices you originally paid. But that could also have implications for what capital gains tax rate you pay if some of the shares were bought more than a year ago while others were bought in the recent year.

Consider the example in Figure 4.8, in which you have bought a total of 400 shares in a company at prices between $46 and $57 over the last two years, and now you are selling 100 of those shares. The default used by the IRS is the *FIFO* (first in, first out) method, which assumes that you sell the shares you bought first and use their purchase price as the cost basis. But this typically gives rise to a higher realized capital gain. In the example, the cost basis from FIFO is $46, with a resulting capital gain of $60 − $46 = $14 per share. An alternative is to use the *high-cost* method, which assumes that you sell the shares with the highest cost basis, which minimizes the realized capital gain. This is generally a better approach for minimizing taxes in the long run. In the example, the realized capital gain would be $60 − $57 = $3 per share. But because this is a short-term gain, you would likely be taxed at a higher rate. You could even use a *specific identification* method, which allows you to pinpoint which specific shares you sold.

In general, choosing to sell the shares with the highest basis is optimal, and I recommend that method as the default. But you might encounter situations in which choosing other lots is more optimal. For example, if the lot with the highest gain was bought in the recent year, the higher capital gains tax rate on short-term gains might be undesirable. Or you might seek the lowest basis when you temporarily face a low tax rate on capital gains and you wish to harvest some capital gains (see further discussion later).

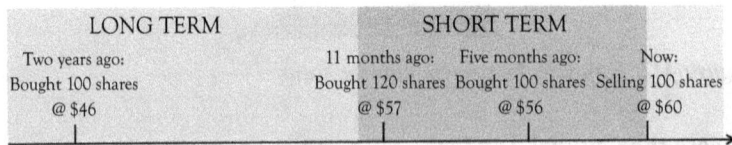

LONG TERM		SHORT TERM		
Two years ago:		11 months ago:	Five months ago:	Now:
Bought 100 shares		Bought 120 shares	Bought 100 shares	Selling 100 shares
@ $46		@ $57	@ $56	@ $60

Figure 4.8 Example of cost basis

Harvest Capital Losses

Realized capital losses can be used to offset realized capital gains and then up to $3,000 in taxable income annually. Any residual realized capital losses can be carried forward indefinitely until they are used up. Figure 4.9 illustrates such loss harvesting.

Figure 4.9 Loss harvesting

With a marginal income tax rate of 30 percent, using capital losses of $3,000 to offset taxable income saves 30% × $3,000 = $900 in taxes that year. This means that some strategic trades every year can save you tens of thousands of dollars in taxes over a lifetime.

Incidentally, the ability to harvest capital losses is only available for securities in a regular brokerage account and not for securities in a tax-favored account. On this basis (and perhaps aided by other tax strategies), one could argue that it is not optimal to keep all the funds in tax-favored accounts even if it were to be possible.

It is perhaps easiest to wait until the end of the year to harvest capital losses. At that time, you can first estimate the net realized gains (or losses) so far that year, making sure you also consider potential losses carried forward from past years. Then you can sell individual securities such that the net realized capital losses equal at least $3,000. For example, if your trades throughout the year have given net realized capital gains of $1,000, you need to sell securities with capital losses of at least $4,000. To identify those securities, you can visit your online brokerage account and browse the list of unrealized capital gains and losses for the securities you hold.

A warning is in order here. The IRS has a wash-sale rule that prevents tax deductions associated with wash-sales, where a wash-sale is defined as the sale of a security at a loss followed by the purchase of a "substantially identical" security within 30 days. Thus, if you sell a security to harvest capital losses, you cannot buy it back for at least 31 days.

Let us conclude with a brief concept test. Suppose that your friend tells you that he does not like the strategy of harvesting capital losses because he believes the investment objective should be to make money, not lose money. How would you respond? Well, even with an objective to make money on his investments, your friend will inevitably lose money on some positions provided that he has many different positions, and then he might as well harvest some losses, right?

Harvest Capital Gains

Recall that the tax rate on realized long-term capital gains drops to zero if you have income less than $45K. Thus, if your income temporarily falls, for example, because you take a sailboat trip around the world as in Figure 4.10, you should consider selling some of your securities that have accumulated long-term capital gains. (There might also be a benefit to selling securities that have accumulated short-term capital gains, but this is likely to be much smaller.)

While the wash-sale rule does not apply to capital-gain harvesting, there are a couple of other pitfalls. First, the zero tax-rate only applies if

Figure 4.10 Sailboat trip around the world

your income, *including* the realized capital gains, is below $45K. Thus, if you expect your income to drop to zero during your trip around the world, you can harvest up to $45K of capital gains. Second, you might have to pay state taxes on the realized capital gains (depending on the state to which you pay taxes), which could offset the benefits.

When You Need Liquidity

Periodically you will likely need to tap into your brokerage accounts for funds, for example, because you need equity for a house purchase, as Figure 4.11 illustrates. If so, you should identify a collection of securities in your brokerage account to sell that would provide the needed liquidity yet collectively have no net capital gain. That way, you avoid realizing capital gains to be taxed. You might even aim to sell a collection of securities that have a net capital loss to be used for harvesting losses that year or a future year.

Figure 4.11 Buying a house

Stock Donations

Most of us regularly donate resources in the form of time and money to charities that we believe contribute positively to the world in which we live. In this section, I show that you might be able to donate money in a more tax-efficient way than simply writing a check or charging your credit card.

I recognize the irony in making tax-efficient charitable donations, in that taxes themselves can also be viewed as a donation to our community. However, you might believe that certain charities help in places that the government largely ignores. Thus, making tax-efficient donations to those charities can be viewed as a way for you to earmark how a greater portion of your donations should be used.

To make your donations more tax-efficient, you can simply donate stock with accumulated long-term capital gains in place of cash (which, in this context, includes writing checks and using debit/credit cards).[5] Figure 4.12 illustrates such a stock donation. Suppose that you own stock that you bought for $2,000 some years ago that currently is valued at $10,000. Furthermore, you have decided to donate $10,000 to *Doctors*

Figure 4.12 Stock donation

---

[5] For stocks that you have held for more than a year, you can claim a deduction for tax purposes that equals the fair market value at the time of donation. For stocks that you have held for less than a year, the deduction is the lower of the fair market value at the time of donation and the cost basis. Thus, it makes less sense to donate stocks that you have held for less than a year.

Without Borders.[6] You can certainly donate cash of $10,000. Alternatively, you can donate the stock, in which case you never have to pay taxes on the accumulated capital gains of $8,000. If you were to sell the stock today and the capital gains tax rate is 15 percent, you might have had to pay capital gains taxes of $8,000 × 15% = $1,200. (Incidentally, the charity does not have to pay taxes on the stock when it is sold.) Of course, if you had instead sold the stock later, you would have deferred the tax payment. Either way, you would likely reduce the true value of your lifetime tax bills by donating stock instead of cash. Thus, you should be able to make even greater charitable donations.[7]

While we are discussing charitable donations, let us take a 10-minute break here so that readers who got this book cheap (or perhaps even free) can go online and donate what they think the book is truly worth to *Doctors Without Borders.*

Back already? Good. Now, let us move on.

Stock Gifts

Just like you may donate stocks to charities, you may gift stocks to individuals, as Figure 4.13 illustrates. If so, the recipient takes over the holding period and is responsible for paying taxes on the accumulated capital gains when (s)he sells the stock, whereas you are off the hook for any capital gains taxes. There are potentially some gift limits that are relevant here, but we will wait to cover that until we get to the estate planning chapter.

Suppose that you give some shares to your daughter that you paid $10 each for three years ago, but they are now priced at $80 each. If your daughter immediately sells the shares, she must pay taxes on the long-term capital gain of $70 each (i.e., the selling price of $80 less the original cost basis of $10). Why would you not instead sell the stock and give your daughter the cash proceeds? You certainly could. But if your

---

[6] You need to pick a charity that is set up to receive stock, and it is easiest to give to those that are already set up by your brokerage firm.

[7] I experienced that the basis for some of my individual stock holdings got lost in the system as I transferred them from one broker to another. Thus, the basis was set to zero. To avoid the hassle of recovering the basis for these stocks, I donated them to a charity.

Figure 4.13 Stock gift

daughter has a lower long-term capital gains tax rate than you, it makes more sense that she pays the capital gains taxes. Perhaps your daughter does not even pay taxes on realized long-term capital gains because her income is sufficiently low, in which case the stock gift helps elude capital gains taxation altogether.

Suppose instead that you paid $100 for each of the shares, meaning that you have accumulated a capital loss of $20 at the time of gifting. If your daughter immediately sells them for $80 each, the rule is that she may not claim a capital loss for tax purposes. Instead, the cost basis for your daughter is adjusted up to the value of the shares at the time of gifting, so she could only claim a capital loss if she sells after the price falls below $80, and that capital loss would be the difference between $80 and the sales price. If she waits to sell after the price has risen above $100, their original cost basis of $80 becomes the basis for the capital gains calculation for tax purposes. Thus, it does not make much sense to gift stocks with an accumulated capital loss; you are better off selling the stock to realize the capital loss for yourself and then gift the cash proceeds.

A word of caution is in order here. Any investment income above $2,300 (in 2023) for a child under the age of 18 (or a full-time student under the age of 24) who is dependent on your tax return is subject to the *kiddie tax*, meaning that investment income exceeding $2,300 is taxed at your tax rate.

In sum, gifting stock reduces the total tax bill across the giver and the recipient if (a) the stock has accumulated capital gains at the time of gifting and (b) the recipient faces a lower tax rate on capital gains than the giver.

Bequest Stock to Your Heirs

When someone inherits stocks (or other investments), the basis is reset to equal the market value upon the original owner's death. Thus, if you inherit stocks with embedded capital gains, the stepped-up basis effectively wipes out these capital gains, and you can sell the stocks immediately without having to pay any capital gains taxes.[8] Figure 4.14 illustrates this.

Consequently, if you intend to leave wealth to your heirs, it makes sense to leave the stocks in your regular brokerage accounts that have accumulated the greatest capital gains. In other words, you should hold on to those Apple and Amazon stocks that you might have bought decades ago (and have since amassed massive capital gains) and pass them on to your heirs as part of their inheritance.

This step-up in basis sounds too good to be true, so much that it is considered a loophole in the tax code. The loophole has allowed wealthy

Figure 4.14 Step-up in basis

---

[8] If you decide to keep the stock, the holding period is deemed to be long term regardless of when the stock was acquired.

families to avoid billions of dollars in taxes for decades. Thus, it is susceptible to political attacks that it might not survive. In the future, it might
be limited to a certain value, or the inheritance might trigger an immediate capital gains tax based on the original basis. If so, new strategies will
undoubtedly take its place, for example, gifting stock with accumulated
capital gains at an advanced age.

Hold a Diversified Portfolio of Individual Securities

I stated earlier that we could obtain an efficient portfolio by simply investing in a combination of the market index and risk-free security. That also
avoids the hassle of investing in many individual securities.

There are, however, potential tax advantages to holding the
individual securities in the index rather than a fund that holds the
individual securities. The investor in Figure 4.15 has recognized this
and is therefore replacing his index funds with individual securities.
Because of firm-specific risk, there is great variation in the return for
the individual securities in the index, with some securities performing
very well and others performing poorly. This variation makes it easier
to pursue the tax strategies discussed earlier. For example, if you wish to

Figure 4.15 Partitioning the fund into individual securities

harvest losses, you can readily do so with a portfolio of individual securities, because there is almost bound to be some that have accumulated capital losses. But if you only hold the market index, you will be unable to harvest losses in most years.

However, it can be challenging to be sufficiently diversified across small stocks by buying these stocks individually. An advantage to using index funds is that it is easier to get exposure to all those small stocks, which have historically performed better than large stocks.

Fortunately, you do not have to avoid investing in index funds altogether to obtain tax benefits. You must only hold enough individual securities so that, at any point in time, your portfolio consists of a blend of positions with capital gains and losses. That way, you can harvest losses at the end of the year or sell combinations of positions with zero capital gain when you need liquidity.

Managing a Nontax-Favored Account— An Extensive Example

To better illustrate the many tax strategies in the previous section, I will present an extensive example. Suppose that at the end of 2018, Tim invested $1,000 in each of the first 20 stocks from the list in Figure 4.16. I have only provided the ticker symbols of the stocks, and the only thing they have in common is that they all have catchy ticker symbols. You may certainly try to guess which industries the stocks belong to (and even the exact companies), but I can assure you that they represent a wide array of industries, and Tim's portfolio should therefore be quite diversified.

I have given prices at the end of 2018, 2019, and 2020 so that we can see how to harvest losses and undertake other opportunistic transactions. Because Tim might invest in other securities than the ones he bought in 2018, I provide price information for another six stocks, also with catchy ticker symbols. Lastly, for comparison, I provide price information for a popular ETF on the S&P 500 index with the ticker symbol SPY.

Let us move forward one year to the end of 2019, as shown in Figure 4.17. Tim has not touched his portfolio so far that year, and now he seeks to harvest some losses to reduce his income taxes. It was overall a

	End 2018	End 2019	One-year return	End 2020	One-year return
BOOM	34.72	44.71	29%	43.25	-3%
BUD	63.63	81.26	28%	69.91	-14%
CAKE	41.68	38.42	-8%	37.06	-4%
CAR	22.48	32.24	43%	37.30	16%
CASH	19.15	36.32	90%	36.56	1%
EAT	41.93	41.55	-1%	56.57	36%
EYES	7.09	5.94	-16%	1.87	-68%
FIZZ	67.42	47.93	-29%	84.90	77%
FUN	43.18	54.25	26%	39.34	-27%
HEAR	14.27	9.45	-34%	21.55	128%
HOG	32.24	36.63	14%	36.70	0%
JOB	0.70	0.39	-44%	1.00	156%
LUV	45.68	53.77	18%	46.61	-13%
MOO	55.55	67.97	22%	77.89	15%
PETS	21.27	22.66	7%	32.06	41%
PLOW	33.85	53.22	57%	42.77	-20%
PZZA	38.67	62.45	62%	84.85	36%
ROCK	35.59	50.44	42%	71.94	43%
SAVE	57.92	40.31	-30%	24.45	-39%
SEED	5.17	5.36	4%	15.19	183%
SHOO	29.62	42.78	44%	35.32	-17%
TAP	53.52	53.29	0%	45.19	-15%
WATT	5.79	1.77	-69%	1.80	2%
WIFI	20.57	10.95	-47%	12.72	16%
XRAY	36.60	56.06	53%	52.36	-7%
ZEUS	14.09	17.80	26%	13.33	-25%
SPY	240.78	315.96	31%	373.88	18%

Invest in these at the end of 2018 (BOOM – SEED)
Invest in these later (SHOO – ZEUS)
ETF for S&P 500 for comparison → SPY

Figure 4.16 List of stocks and prices

	End 2018 Buy	End 2019 Value before transactions	Gain/Loss since purchase	In %	Sell (if loss >$100)	Harvested losses	Buy	Donate	Value after transactions
BOOM	$1,000	$1,288	$288	29%	$0				$1,288
BUD	$1,000	$1,277	$277	28%	$0				$1,277
CAKE	$1,000	$922	-$78	-8%	$0				$922
CAR	$1,000	$1,434	$434	43%	$0				$1,434
CASH	$1,000	$1,897	$897	90%	$0			$1,000	$897
EAT	$1,000	$991	-$9	-1%	$0				$991
EYES	$1,000	$837	-$163	-16%	$837	-$163			
FIZZ	$1,000	$711	-$289	-29%	$711	-$289			
FUN	$1,000	$1,256	$256	26%	$0				$1,256
HEAR	$1,000	$662	-$338	-34%	$662	-$338			
HOG	$1,000	$1,136	$136	14%	$0				$1,136
JOB	$1,000	$557	-$443	-44%	$557	-$443			
LUV	$1,000	$1,177	$177	18%	$0				$1,177
MOO	$1,000	$1,224	$224	22%	$0				$1,224
PETS	$1,000	$1,065	$65	7%	$0				$1,065
PLOW	$1,000	$1,572	$572	57%	$0				$1,572
PZZA	$1,000	$1,615	$615	62%	$0				$1,615
ROCK	$1,000	$1,417	$417	42%	$0				$1,417
SAVE	$1,000	$696	-$304	-30%	$696	-$304			
SEED	$1,000	$1,037	$37	4%	$0				$1,037
SHOO							$1,411		$1,411
TAP							$1,411		$1,411
WATT							$1,411		$1,411
WIFI							$1,411		$1,411
XRAY							$1,411		$1,411
ZEUS							$1,411		$1,411
	$20,000	$22,772	$2,772		$3,464	-$1,536	$8,464	$1,000	$26,772

Figure 4.17 Actions at the end of 2019

superb year for the market, with the S&P going up more than 30 percent! Yet, some of Tim's securities have experienced capital losses, and he decides to sell all of those with a capital loss of at least $100, which includes five securities with total capital losses of $1,536. He could have sold another two stocks with a capital loss of less than $100, but he decided it wouldn't make much of a difference.

Tim has an income of $100,000 and an employment tax rate of 30 percent, so he should ordinarily pay $30,000 in taxes.[9] Harvesting capital gains losses of $1,536 reduces his taxable income to $98,464 and his taxes to $29,539. Thus, he was able to save $30,000 − $29,539 = $461 in taxes. This can also be calculated more directly as 30% × $1,536 = $461.

Had the market overall not performed as well or had Tim invested in a larger portfolio, he could have harvested more losses for greater tax savings. The maximum capital loss that the IRS would allow Tim to claim against his income in 2019 is $3,000, in which case the tax savings would have been 30% × $3,000 = $900.

Note that had Tim invested all his money in the market index fund SPY instead, he would not have been able to harvest any losses. This illustrates the benefit of investing in individual securities rather than in an index.

Tim receives $3,464 from selling the securities in connection with harvesting losses. In addition, he has saved another $5,000 that he wishes to invest in stocks. He cannot buy back the securities he just sold to comply with the wash-sale rule. Instead, he spreads the total of $3,464 + $5,000 = $8,464 across six new securities, investing $8,464/6 = $1,411 in each.

Finally, Tim wishes to make a charitable donation of $1,000 at the end of 2019. Thus, he identifies the position with the greatest percentage gain, CASH, which has risen in value from $1,000 to $1,897, or 90 percent, and donates $1,000 worth of that position. He originally paid about $1,000/1.9 = $526 for that stock, and the remainder $474 is capital gains. If he were to sell that stock and then donate the proceeds,

---

[9] I assume for simplicity that the marginal and average employment tax rates are the same in this example and other examples in the book. In general, the marginal tax rate is more relevant than the average tax rate.

he would have had to pay capital gains taxes of about $474 × 15% = $71, and he would only have had $1,000 − $71 = $929 left to donate. If he alternatively donated $1,000 from his cash balance, he would still have the $1,000 of stock that he would have to pay capital gains taxes on in the future.

Let us move forward another year to the end of 2020, as shown in Figure 4.18. It was another superb year for the stock market, with the S&P 500 increasing 18 percent. Yet, as the figure shows, Tim was able to harvest another $925 of capital losses by selling positions with capital losses of at least $100. He spends the proceeds, along with another $5,000 of savings, to invest in the securities he sold at the end of 2019. He certainly could have bought other securities as well, but Tim wishes to keep a portfolio with catchy ticker symbols and buying these securities is no longer in violation of the wash-sale rule. Lastly, he donates part of his position in SEED, which has increased an astounding 194 percent since he bought it so that most of the stock donation represents capital gains.

What if Tim needed more liquidity in 2020? He certainly did not have to invest the sale proceeds of $4,307 and the additional $5,000 that year. Furthermore, he could liquidate additional stock. If so, he should

	End 2020								
	Value before transactions	Gain/Loss last year	Gain/Loss since purchase	In %	Sell (if loss >$100)	Harvested losses	Buy	Donate	Value after transactions
BOOM	$1,246	-$42	$246	25%	$0				$1,246
BUD	$1,099	-$178	$99	10%	$0				$1,099
CAKE	$889	-$33	-$111	-11%	$889	-$111			$0
CAR	$1,659	$225	$659	66%	$0				$1,659
CASH	$903	$6	-$97	-10%	$0				$903
EAT	$1,349	$358	$349	35%	$0				$1,349
EYES							$1,861		$1,861
FIZZ							$1,861		$1,861
FUN	$911	-$345	-$89	-9%	$0				$911
HEAR							$1,861		$1,861
HOG	$1,138	$2	$138	14%	$0				$1,138
JOB							$1,861		$1,861
LUV	$1,020	-$157	$20	2%	$0				$1,020
MOO	$1,402	$178	$402	40%	$0				$1,402
PETS	$1,507	$442	$507	51%	$0				$1,507
PLOW	$1,263	-$309	$263	26%	$0				$1,263
PZZA	$2,194	$579	$1,194	119%	$0				$2,194
ROCK	$2,021	$604	$1,021	102%	$0				$2,021
SAVE							$1,861		$1,861
SEED	$2,938	$1,901	$1,938	194%	$0			$1,000	$1,938
SHOO	$1,165	-$246	-$246	-17%	$1,165	-$246			
TAP	$1,196	-$214	-$214	-15%	$1,196	-$214			
WATT	$1,435	$24	$24	2%	$0				$1,435
WIFI	$1,639	$228	$228	16%	$0				$1,639
XRAY	$1,318	-$93	-$93	-7%	$0				$1,318
ZEUS	$1,056	-$354	-$354	-25%	$1,056	-$354			
	$29,349	$2,577	$5,885		$4,307	-$925	$9,307	$1,000	$33,349

Figure 4.18 Actions at the end of 2020

strive to sell the stock with a net capital gain close to zero. Reasonable alternatives include the following:

- Sell FUN at $911; capital loss = $89
- Sell XRAY at $1,318; capital loss = $93
- Sell LUV at $1,020; capital gain = $20
- Sell WATT at $1,435; capital gain = $24
- Sell BUD at $1,099; capital gain = $99

Selling all of these would give proceeds of $5,783 and a net capital loss of $39. Thus, the capital gains tax consequence from this would be minimal. In this case, it would actually provide a slight additional tax break.

CHAPTER 5

Retirement Accounts

We can obviously all save money in regular bank and brokerage accounts, whether it be for a new car or other future investments. This chapter discusses special accounts for the purpose of saving toward retirement. These accounts, humorously illustrated in Figure 5.1, have two advantages. First, they provide discipline in our saving behavior by enforcing and enticing regular contributions and by discouraging early withdrawals. Second, they typically come with substantial tax benefits.

I start with a brief discussion of Social Security, which is not strictly an account, but rather a savings system, whereby the federal government taxes us in exchange for promises of future payouts. Furthermore,

Figure 5.1 Retirement account

most employers, but unfortunately not all, provide retirement plans that complement social security benefits. Finally, irrespective of whether you qualify for social security benefits and whether your employer provides a retirement plan, you might supplement with an individual retirement account (IRA) and/or a self-employment retirement account.

The main objectives for this chapter are:

- Explore how individuals can save for retirement, including via:
  o Social Security;
  o Employer-sponsored retirement plans; and
  o Individual retirement accounts (IRAs).
- Learn the embedded benefits of various retirement plans/ accounts and how to leverage those benefits.

Social Security

As Figure 5.2 indicates, *Social Security* is a federal program that taxes individuals during their working years and pays those individuals when they have retired. Most individuals with a reasonable income qualify for social security benefits after working for 10 years, and the amount they receive upon retirement depends on the years of employment and the average

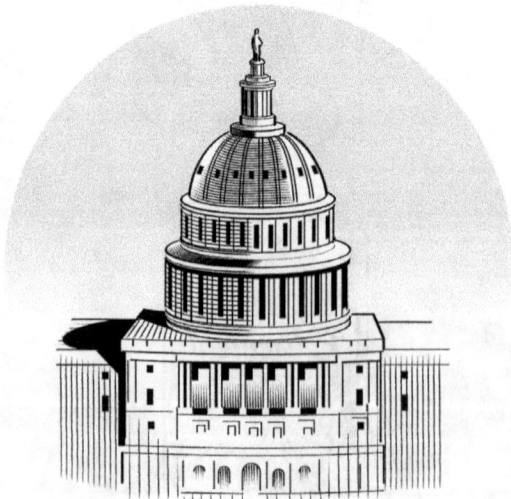

Figure 5.2 The federal government as the provider of social security

income.[1] The average annual benefit was about $22,000 as of 2023, and the maximum was about $44,000 (and higher if the start of the payments is postponed). It is quite likely future inflation-adjusted benefits will be lower still because the program runs short on funds. Thus, you should not rely solely on social security benefits for a comfortable retirement.

You can start receiving benefits at any age between 62 up and age 70, and the periodic benefits will be higher the longer you delay the start of the benefits. Figure 5.3 illustrates this for those with a full retirement age (FRA) of 67, which pertains to individuals born in 1960 or after. Whether you start early depends primarily on your other income sources and your life expectancy; if you have other income sources and expect to live a long life, you should delay the start of the benefits.

You may also be eligible for spousal benefits if you are married, formerly married, divorced, or widowed. There are many relevant rules and strategies here, and I refer to other sources for complete coverage. In any event, here are some basic rules:

- You must be at least 62 years old or have a child under your care to receive spousal benefits.
- The maximum spousal benefit is 50 percent of the other spouse's benefit estimated at FRA, or 100 percent if you are widowed.
- If you have your own benefit, you will receive the larger of your benefit and the spousal benefit.
- If you are divorced, you must have been married for at least 10 years and currently be unmarried to be eligible for spousal benefits.

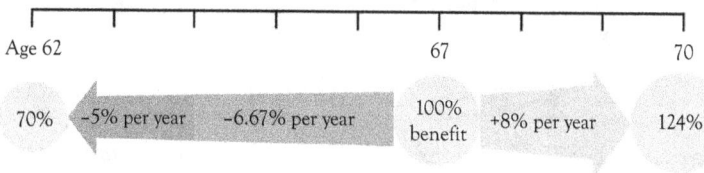

Figure 5.3 Social security benefits and age

---

[1] You can estimate Social Security benefits on this website: www.ssa.gov/OACT/quickcalc/.

Part of the social security benefits may be taxed, but essentially only if you also have other sources of income. To determine whether the social security benefits will be taxed, you estimate *combined income* as the sum of (i) adjusted gross income, (ii) tax-exempt interest, and (iii) half of the social security benefits. For 2023, individual filers could pay income tax on up to 50 percent of the social security benefits if the combined income is between $25,000 and $34,000 and up to 85 percent of the social security benefits if the combined income exceeds $34,000. For those married filing jointly, the thresholds are a little higher at $32,000 and $44,000.

Employer-Sponsored Retirement Plans

Most employers, ranging from city governments to large corporations, as illustrated in Figure 5.4, offer retirement plans to their employees. There are two types of plans: defined benefit and defined contribution. Defined benefit plans are gradually disappearing from the private sector and are now mostly offered by state and local governments.

Figure 5.4 *Large corporations as providers of retirement plans*

Defined Benefit Plans

Defined benefit plans provide guaranteed periodic amounts when you retire based on the years of employment and the income, and you might have to work for a certain number of years before you qualify for the benefits. The advantage for the employee is that the retirement income is quite certain, though not particularly high. If you have a defined benefit plan, you do not have to make many decisions, and much of this chapter might not pertain to your situation. But it could still be wise to supplement with an IRA, especially if the defined benefits are projected to be low or you intend to make some investments in securities anyway.

Defined Contribution Plans

In *defined contribution plans*, the employer and/or employee contribute to the employee's IRA. The employee then decides, within certain constraints, how the money is invested and how the total investment value is withdrawn during retirement. This quickly becomes very complex, which is why we need to dive deeper into the many decisions and issues related to defined contribution plans.

There are several types of defined contribution plans, including:

- 401(k), which is very common in the corporate world;
- 403(b), which is used by nonprofit organizations and educational institutions;
- 457(b), which is used primarily by state and local governments, often as an additional plan; and
- Thrift Savings Plan (TSP), which is used by the federal government.

Generally, your plan is determined by the employer type, but the plans are quite similar. A private, for-profit firm will likely offer a 401(k) plan, while a nonprofit or government might offer a 403(b) and/or a 457 plan. Many large government employers (like the University of Iowa) offer both a 403(b) and a 457(b) plan, in which case the employees have the added benefit of being able to contribute the maximum amounts to both.

The employer might contribute a certain amount every pay period, while the employee may elect to contribute via a deduction from her paycheck. For example, the employer might contribute 5 percent of the employee's income (which means that the contribution comes in addition to the regular income), while the employee might choose to contribute 5 percent of the income (which means that the contribution is deducted from the income).[2] The employer contribution might also provide a matching contribution based on what the employee elects to contribute. For example, the employer might match 50 percent of what the employee contributes, which obviously makes employee contributions more appealing.

The SECURE 2.0 Act of 2022 requires employers to automatically enroll employees in 401(k) and 403(b) plans adopted after January 1, 2023, with a minimum contribution rate of 3 percent and a maximum of 10 percent. The contribution rate must increase by 1 percent per year up to a minimum of 10 percent and a maximum of 15 percent.

The contributions are generally pretax (which is effectively the same as the contributions being tax deductible).[3] Thus, with a monthly paycheck before taxes of $5,000 and an employment tax rate of 20 percent, the employer might contribute 5% × $5,000 = $250, the employee might contribute another 5% × $5,000 = $250, and the amount paid out to the employee after taxes would be ($5,000 − $250) × (100% − 20%) = $3,800.

In 2023, the employee may contribute up to a maximum of $22,500 (plus $7,500 of catch-up contributions if the employee is above 50 years old, for a total of $30,000) or 100 percent of the employee's compensation, and the maximum contribution across the employer and employee is $66,000 ($73,500 if the employee is above 50).[4] In the extreme case, an employee above 50 with both 403(b) and 457 plans and high income might contribute a total of $73,500 + $30,000 = $103,500. However,

---

[2] In a 401(k), the employer contribution could also depend on the profit level of the corporation. Naturally, this is not possible for other plans because they are offered by nonprofit organizations.

[3] The plans might also be available in so-called Roth form, in which case the contribution is after tax. I have chosen to postpone the discussion of Roth plans until the section on individual retirement plans, where they are more commonly used. Note, however, that until new rules take effect in 2024, the Roth forms of 401(k), 403(b), and 457(b) plans have withdrawal rules that match those of standard 401(k), 403(b), and 457(b) plans, and not those of Roth IRA plans.

[4] The SECURE Act of 2022 stipulates that, starting in 2024, those who make more than $145,000 must deposit catch-up contributions to a Roth 401(k) account. Furthermore, starting in 2025, individuals between the ages of 60 and 63 can make catch-up contributions of $10,000.

most employees contribute less because they (i) have lower salaries, (ii) have access to only one of the 401(k), 403(b), and 457 plans, (iii) are under 50 years old, or (iv) choose not to contribute the maximum amount, perhaps because they do not understand the benefits.

The employee can choose how the contribution is invested from a menu of mutual funds and ETFs. Some of these funds come with high fees, so you should make sure to select those with low fees, and if they are not available, you should complain to your employer.[5]

The investments accrue on a tax-deferred basis. For 401(k) and 403(b) plans, there is a 10 percent penalty for withdrawing funds unless (i) you retire at the age of 55 and subsequently withdraw the funds, (ii) you have reached the age of 59½, or (iii) you have suffered hardship, for example, you have uncovered medical expenses.[6] When you have reached the age of 73, you are required to withdraw a minimum amount each year called the *Required Minimum Distribution* (RMD), even on 457 plans.[7] In 2033, the age requirement will increase from 73 to 75.

Assuming that the contributions were made pretax, the withdrawals from the retirement accounts are subject to employment income taxes, even though much of the value stems from investment income. You might ask: what is the tax benefit then? The benefit stems from the absence of investment income taxes. Let me illustrate with a simple example.

Suppose that you have an income of $1,000, an employment income tax rate of 25 percent, and an investment income tax rate of 15 percent. After

---

[5] It is only in the last decade or so that University of Iowa employees gained access to low-cost Vanguard funds in their retirement accounts after a push from informed and insistent employees.

[6] Your employer might also allow you to borrow from your 401(k). To avoid a penalty, you should pay back the funds within five years and use the funds for a first-time purchase of a primary residence or your children's education. I recommend against such loans because you might find it hard to return the money.

[7] There is a "still-working" exception that allows the RMD to be delayed beyond the age of 73 provided that (i) you are still working, (ii) the retirement account is sponsored by the current employer, and (iii) you do not own more than 5 percent of the employer. For example, the University of Iowa has no mandatory retirement age, and faculty who choose to work after they have reached 73 do not have to start withdrawing from their University of Iowa retirement accounts until they retire.

paying the employment income tax rate of $250, you have $750 to invest. If the investment doubles in value, you end up with $1,500, or **$1,275** after investment income taxes of $225. This is illustrated in Figure 5.5.

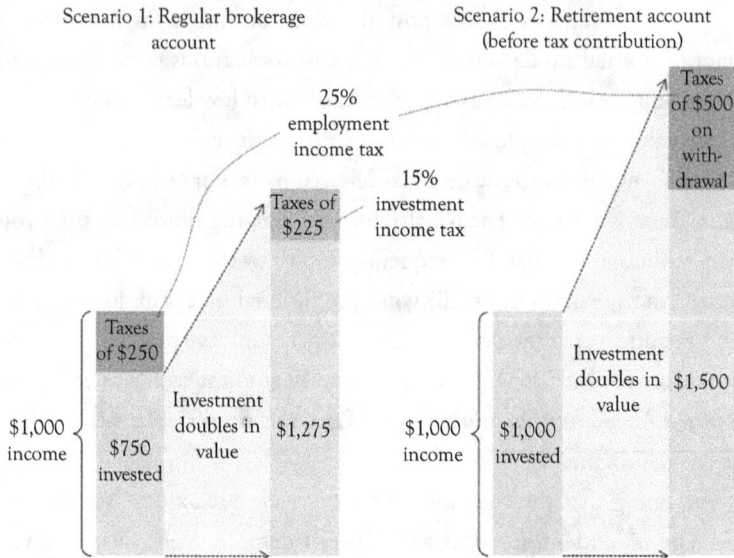

Figure 5.5 Growth in a regular brokerage account versus in a retirement account

Suppose instead that you can contribute the entire pretax income of $1,000 to a retirement account. If the investment doubles in value, you have $2,000, or **$1,500** after employment income taxes of $500 on the withdrawal.

In a more extensive example later, I will also show what happens if the employment income tax changes over time or the account is a so-called Roth type, in which you can contribute after-tax money that is allowed to grow without investment income taxes. Just bear with me.

Individual Retirement Plans

In addition to an employer-sponsored retirement plan, individuals like the person in Figure 5.6 may open an IRA. It comes in two forms, the traditional IRA and the Roth IRA, and unlike employer-sponsored plans, they do not restrict the securities in which to invest.

Figure 5.6 An individual who can open an IRA

With the *traditional IRA*, you contribute pretax money and pay employment income tax on later withdrawals. This is like the bulk of employer-sponsored retirement plans that we discussed in the prior subsection. With the *Roth IRA* (named after Senator William Roth of Delaware, who sponsored the relevant legislation), you contribute post-tax money and pay no taxes on later withdrawals. Both types are exempt from investment income taxes.

However, you only qualify for these plans if your Modified Adjusted Gross Income (MAGI) is below certain thresholds.[8] For single filers in 2023, the thresholds for full contributions are:

- $73,000 for a traditional IRA for those with an employer-sponsored plan; and
- $138,000 for a Roth IRA.

For individuals filing jointly in 2023, the thresholds for full contributions are:

- $116,000 for a traditional IRA for those with an employer-sponsored plan;

---

[8] In short, MAGI equals your gross income adjusted for various deductions, and you can find calculators online to estimate this.

- $228,000 for a traditional IRA for those whose spouse has an employer-sponsored plan; and
- $228,000 for a Roth IRA.

If you qualify, you may contribute up to $6,500 across both types, or $7,500 if you are above 50 years old.[9] As Figures 5.7, 5.8, 5.9, and 5.10

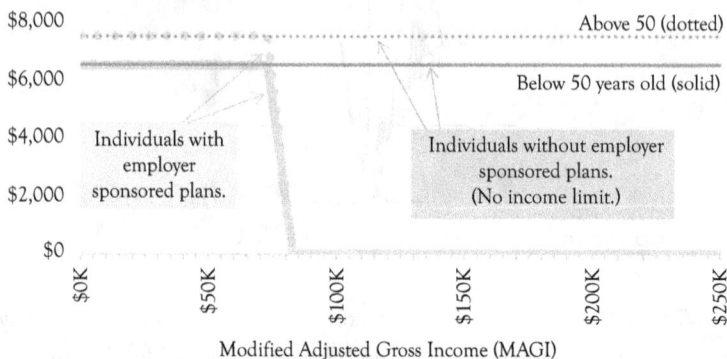

Figure 5.7 Traditional IRA contribution limits for single filers

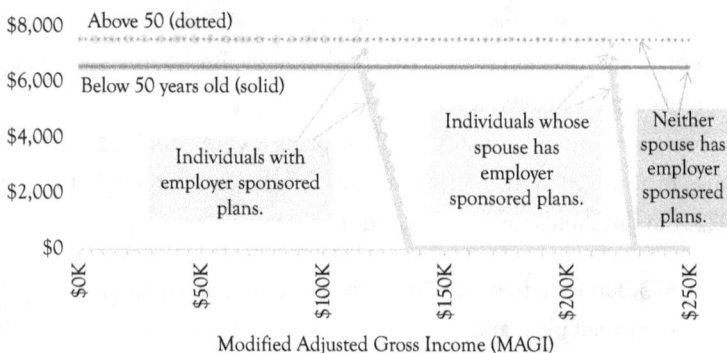

Figure 5.8 Traditional IRA contribution limits for married filing jointly

---

[9] Contributions to a *nondeductible traditional IRA* are not subject to the income limit. In that case, you cannot deduct the contribution from your taxes, meaning that the contribution is after tax. You also face taxes on later withdrawals, but there are still no investment income taxes. Thus, this might not make sense. However, some individuals proceed to transfer the funds to a Roth account to create a so-called "backdoor Roth IRA." There are some complicated tax rules and calculations that pertain to that transfer, especially because the IRAs end up having a mix of deductible and nondeductible funds that cannot be disentangled, so beware.

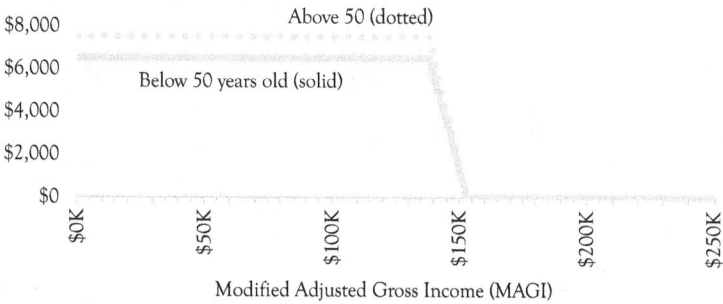

Figure 5.9 Roth IRA contribution limits for single filers

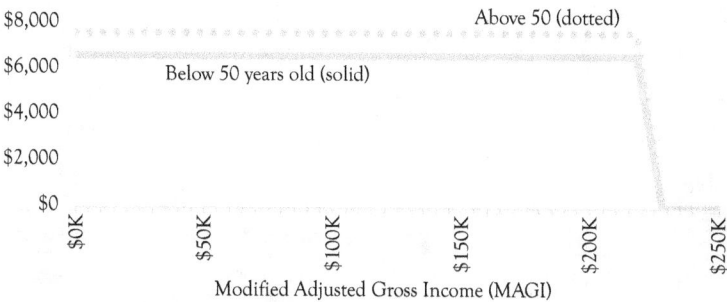

Figure 5.10 Roth IRA contribution limits for married filing jointly

show, partial contributions are allowed for income levels right above the thresholds for full contributions.

There are also a couple of other differences between traditional and Roth IRAs, both of which favor the latter. Table 5.1 summarizes these differences. First, Roth IRA has more flexibility for penalty-free withdrawals. The minimum age for penalty-free withdrawals is 59.5 for both types unless you have qualified expenses for medical treatment, education, or other financial hardship. However, the age constraint does not pertain to the original contributions for Roth IRAs, as emphasized in Table 5.2. Thus, if you originally contributed $5,000 to a Roth IRA that has since grown in value to $12,000, you can withdraw $5,000 any time without facing a penalty. A slight caveat that counts against Roth IRAs is that for earnings to be withdrawn penalty-free after the age of 59.5, you must have contributed to the Roth IRA (or another Roth IRA that you own) at least five tax years prior to the withdrawal.

Table 5.1 Traditional versus Roth IRA

	Traditional IRA	Roth IRA
Contributions	Before tax	After tax
Withdrawals	Taxed as income	Tax-free
Income limit	None, except if you have an employer-sponsored plan, in which case the income limit is given in earlier graphs	Income limit is given in earlier graphs
Minimum age for penalty-free withdrawals	59.5 (or earlier if you qualify for an exception)	Contributions: **None** Earnings: 59.5 (or earlier if you qualify for an exception)
Required minimum distribution (RMD)	Starting at age 73 (75 in 2033 onwards)	**None**
Contribution limit	$6,500 across both types ($7,500 if over 50), but no more than your taxable income	

Table 5.2 Withdrawals from retirement accounts

		<59 ½ years old	≥59 ½ years old
Traditional IRA	Contributions	**Penalty** (some exceptions)	Free withdrawals
	Earnings		
Roth IRA	Contributions	Free withdrawals	
	Earnings	**Penalty** (some exceptions)	Free (if plan has been open ≥5 years)

Second, the RMD for a traditional IRA starts at the age of 73 (age 75 starting in 2033), while there is no RMD for the Roth IRA. The absence of RMD is potentially beneficial because it allows you to keep the money in your IRA to grow tax-free longer, assuming, of course, that you do not need the money yet. Furthermore, many individuals estimate the RMD incorrectly or forget to withdraw the RMD, which could result in a hefty 25 percent penalty on the amount that was not withdrawn as it should have been.

You can choose to transfer funds from your traditional IRA to a Roth IRA whenever you want, but not the other way around. However, when you convert any pretax funds from the traditional IRA to a Roth IRA, you must pay income taxes on the full transfer value. Thus, you should only consider this if your current employment income tax rate is lower than you expect it to be in the future. Note also that the taxable income from the conversion might push you into a higher tax bracket.

Some of you might have detected an apparent opportunity to dodge the age rule for penalty-free withdrawals of contributions in traditional IRAs by transferring the funds to a Roth IRA immediately before the withdrawals. Not so. The funds that you transfer from a traditional IRA to a Roth IRA must remain in the Roth IRA for at least five tax years before they can be withdrawn penalty-free.[10]

The discussion of differences between traditional and Roth IRAs leads to the question: Which account type should you choose?

Many argue that the choice depends on what is likely to happen to your employment income tax rate. Because the taxation occurs later for the traditional IRA than for the Roth IRA, a declining income tax rate favors the traditional IRA. Some individuals face such a declining tax rate because they have a lower income during retirement than during the working years or because they move to a state with lower taxes on withdrawals.[11] But individuals often face a surprisingly high income during retirement, especially if their retirement accounts are subject to RMD.[12] Complicating things further, legislators might increase employment income taxes to fund other programs, like Social Security.[13] A common recommendation then is to use both a traditional IRA and a Roth IRA as a hedge against the uncertainty in your future tax rate.

As a rule of thumb, I favor the Roth IRA for at least some of the IRA contributions for three reasons, the two first of which I noted earlier, so

---

[10] How do you know exactly which funds are withdrawn from the Roth IRA? The IRS states that the order of withdrawals is: first contributions, then conversions (with older conversions preceding newer conversions), and finally earnings.

[11] Some states simply have no income taxes at all, and a few states exempt withdrawals from income taxation.

[12] There is an interesting circularity here. A declining tax rate makes the traditional IRA more appealing, but the RMD of the traditional IRA might push you into a higher tax bracket.

[13] Because you can convert from a traditional IRA to a Roth IRA, but not the other way around, the traditional IRA provides more flexibility in case of a sudden change in your tax rate.

there is some redundancy. First, the Roth IRA has no penalty for early withdrawals of the original contributions. Thus, if you might have a sudden need for liquidity, for example, to buy a house, the Roth IRA is better. I must admit, though, that I would generally advice strongly against withdrawing from your retirement account before you have retired, so perhaps this reason is less important. Second, there is no RMD on the Roth IRA, allowing you to keep your money in the account for a longer time and produce more tax-free investment income, while also keeping the employment income tax rate low. This is particularly relevant if you expect to have a substantial IRA at the time of retirement. Third, the Roth IRA allows you to shield more pretax income. For example, if your IRA contribution limit is $6,500 and your employment income tax rate is 30 percent, you can contribute $6,500 of your pretax income to a traditional IRA or $6,500/(1 − 30%) = $9,286 to a Roth IRA. I will explain further in my later example. In any event, it is only relevant if you bump into the maximum allowable contribution and would like to invest even more in your retirement accounts.

However, I also recommend a traditional IRA for some IRA contributions because it allows you to take advantage of temporary drops in your tax rate. So, if you do not work for a year (because you are unemployed or take a year off), you can transfer funds from your traditional IRA to a Roth IRA at a low tax rate, and then you are off the hook for further taxes on these funds.

Let me conclude this subsection with Table 5.3, which summarizes the contribution limits for the employer-sponsored and individual plans.

Table 5.3 Summary of contribution limits

Contribution limits			
401(k)/403(b)/457 from employer	**401(k)/403(b)/457 from employee**	**Traditional IRA**	**Roth IRA**
	$22,500 ($30,000 if over 50)	$6,500 ($7,500 if over 50)	
Total is limited to $66,000 ($73,500 if over 50), but no more than your compensation. If both a 403(b) and a 457(b) are available, employees might contribute another $22,500 ($30,000 if over 50), making the total limit $88,500 ($103,500 if over 50).		Additional limits depend on your income level and whether you have an employer-sponsored plan.	

Self-Employed/Small Business Retirement Plans

There are several available plans for self-employed individuals and small businesses like the one in Figure 5.11. Of these, the solo 401(k) is generally preferable because it allows the greatest contribution and does not suffer from any clear disadvantages.

A *solo 401(k)* is an individual 401(k) for a business owner with no employees. Thus, the individual serves both as the employer and the employee. The contribution limits in 2023 are:

- In the role as employer: up to 20 percent of net income.
- In the role as employee: $22,500 (or $30,000 if over 50), though no more than the compensation.
- Both roles combined: $66,000 or $73,500 if over 50 years old.

Like many other plans, a solo 401(k) can be structured as a traditional version or as a Roth version.

A *SIMPLE (Savings Incentive Match Plan for Employees) IRA* is designed to be cheap and easy for small businesses. In 2023, the contribution limit is $15,500, or $19,000 for individuals above 50 years old.

A *SEP-IRA* allows total contributions of 25 percent of compensation, but no more than $66,000 in 2023, or $73,500 for individuals above 50 years old.

Suppose that you are a 52-year-old self-employed individual and have earned an income of $100,000. The maximum contributions toward various plans are then given in Table 5.4. At about $49,000, the solo 401(k) allows almost double the contribution of the second-best alternative.

Figure 5.11 *A small business that can provide unique retirement plans*

Table 5.4 An example of maximum contributions

	Employer contribution	Employee contribution	Total
Solo (401(k))	20% × $100,000 × 92.35% = $18,587 (only 92.35% of self-employment income is generally subject to tax)	$30,000	$48,587
SIMPLE IRA		$19,000	$19,000
SEP-IRA	25% × $100,000 = $25,000		$25,000
Traditional IRA		$7,500	$7,500

Extensions

Spousal IRAs

Special rules apply to spouses, as illustrated in Figure 5.12. A spousal IRA looks like any other IRA; it will just be listed as an IRA or Roth IRA. What makes it special is that the owner, let us call him Owen, has little or no income, perhaps because he is a stay-at-home dad, yet the IRA receives substantial contributions. This violates our earlier discussion that you cannot contribute more than your income. Well, there is a loophole for spouses filing jointly. If Owen's spouse, let us call her Sidney, makes sufficient to contribute to both her and Owen's account, she may do so.

Here are the constraints:

- The married couple must file their taxes jointly.
- The income limits discussed earlier for individuals who file jointly apply.

Figure 5.12 Spouses are subject to special IRA rules

- Each spouse can make a maximum annual contribution of $6,500 in 2023 ($7,500 for those above 50), just like for other individuals. The tweak is that the earned income requirement can be fulfilled mostly or entirely by one spouse. Thus, if both spouses are less than 50 years old and one spouse has no income, the other spouse would have to make at least $13,000 for each to contribute $6,500.

Excess IRA Contributions

You might make the mistake of contributing more than the legal limit to your IRA. If so, you should correct the mistake by withdrawing the excess contribution plus any income earned on that excess contribution by the due date for your tax returns. The earned income on the excess contribution should be calculated using the net income attributable (NIA) formula: Excess contribution × ((ACB − AOB)/AOB). IRS defines the *adjusted opening balance* (AOB) as the previous IRA balance plus all contributions (including the excess one), consolidations, and transfers into the account since you made the excess contribution, and the *adjusted closing balance* (ACB) as the current value IRA balance minus all distributions, consolidations, and transfers since the excess contribution.

Suppose that you could contribute a maximum of $6,500 to your IRA but contributed $8,500 by mistake, such that the excess contribution is $2,000. Furthermore, suppose that the IRA balance was $100,000 right before you made the contribution, and it is now $112,000. In that case, AOB = $100,000 + $8,500 = $108,500 and ACB = $112,000, and the earned income from the excess contribution is: $2,000 × ($112,000 − $108,500)/$108,500 = $65. Thus, you should withdraw $2,000 + $65 = $2,065 from the IRA.

If you fail to make the withdrawal, you will be slapped with a tax penalty of 6 percent per year that the excess remains in the IRA, though it cannot exceed 6 percent of all your IRAs at the end of the tax year. In the example earlier, you would pay an excise tax of 6% × $2,000 = $120 each year until the issue is resolved.

Saver's Credit

The retirement savings contribution credit ("saver's credit") is a tax credit up to $1,000 ($2,000 if married filing jointly) for mid- and low-income taxpayers who contribute to retirement accounts. Note that a tax credit reduces your taxes by the full amount of the credit and, thus, is much better than a tax deduction (which only reduces your taxes by the tax deduction multiplied by your marginal tax rate).

Here are the requirements for the saver's credit:

- You are 18 or older by the end of the tax year, not a full-time student, and not claimed as a dependent on another individual's tax return.
- You contribute to a retirement account.
- You make less than the adjusted gross income (AGI) thresholds. Table 5.5 shows the credit as a fraction of your contribution for various levels of AGI (up to the maximum of $1,000, or $2,000 if you file jointly).

For example, if you made $20,000 during 2023, your employer contributed $1,000 to a 401K plan, and you contributed $500 to an IRA, you qualify for a tax credit of 50% × ($1,000 + $500) = $750.

To claim the credit, you need to complete IRS Form 8880 if you are preparing your tax return manually. It is worth the effort if you qualify.

Starting in 2027, the *saver's credit* will be replaced with the *saver's match*. Instead of the nonrefundable tax credit, the federal government will deposit a matching contribution directly into the taxpayer's retirement account of choice (though it cannot be a Roth account). Also, the phase-out ranges are adjusted and expanded.

Table 5.5 *Saver's credit as a fraction of contribution*

Fraction of contribution	Married filing jointly	Head of household	Other filers
50%	AGI ≤ $43,500	AGI ≤ $32,625	AGI ≤ $21,750
20%	$43,501 – $47,500	$32,626 – $35,625	$21,751 – $23,750
10%	$47,501 – $73,000	$35,626 – $54,750	$23,751 – $36,500
0%	AGI > $73,000	AGI > $54,750	AGI > $36,500

More on RMDs

The IRS defines RMD to equal the account value divided by life expectancy, and it is roughly 4 percent of the value initially and then increasing, as illustrated in Figure 5.13.[14]

If you have multiple retirement accounts, you should first calculate the RMD for each retirement account. If you have multiple IRAs, you can sum up the RMDs for these accounts and withdraw the total amount from one or more of the accounts as you desire. The same pertains to multiple 403(b) accounts. But for other types of retirement plans, including 401(k), 457(b), and TSPs, the RMDs must be withdrawn *separately* from each account.

The RMD rules can be confusing and are occasionally updated. Thus, if you have retirement accounts with RMDs and are approaching the age of 73, you should pay close attention to the rules and consider getting professional assistance. Failure to comply with the RMD rules in a timely manner can lead to a stiff 25 percent penalty on the amount that should have been withdrawn. If you fail to make an RMD withdrawal on time, you should fix the mistake as soon as possible by making the withdrawal and apply for a waiver of the penalty with the IRS. Chances are good that you get a waiver if you made a "reasonable error."

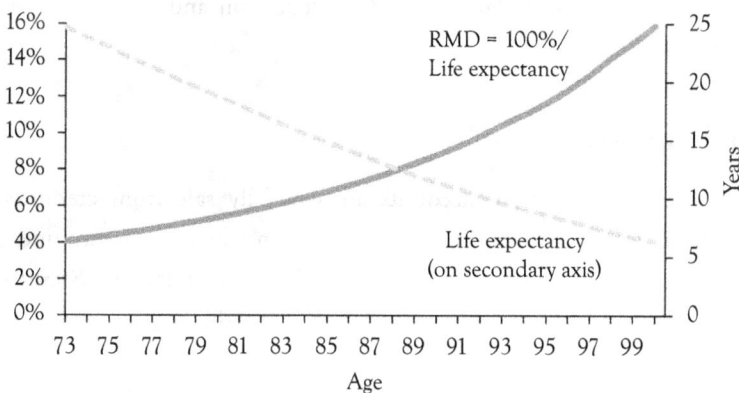

Figure 5.13 RMD and life expectancy

---

[14] You can readily find RMD calculators online to make more precise estimates. Note that the IRS has several life expectancy tables that apply to different situations.

Qualified Charitable Distributions

The Qualified Charitable Distribution (QCD) rule allows individuals who are at least 73 years old (75 starting in 2033) to send funds directly from their IRA to qualified charitable organizations without recording the funds as income for tax purposes. QCDs also count toward RMDs. There are a few constraints:

- The individual must be at least 73 years old on the date of the QCD.
- The funds must go directly from the IRA to the charity.
- The cap is $100,000 per person per year.
- Nondeductible contributions in the IRA do not qualify. (This is only an issue for the minority of individuals who have made such nondeductible contributions.)

The rule can also be applied for Roth IRAs, but because distributions from Roth IRAs are already tax-free and there is no RMD on Roth IRAs, there is no benefit.

You might argue that you could just take a regular IRA distribution, donate that money to charity, and finally claim a tax deduction on the donation. However, that strategy might not be equally effective, for example, because you claim a standard deduction and do not itemize deductions.

Creditor Protection

The assets in retirement accounts are generally safe from creditors. However, there are exceptions that depend on whether the retirement accounts are protected by the Employee Retirement Income Security Act (ERISA). The rules are complicated, and this section offers an incomplete overview.

ERISA covers most employer-sponsored retirement plans, including 401(k) plans and some 403(b) plans, and offers strong protection against creditors. Only the federal government (primarily the IRS) and ex-spouses can make claims on assets in those accounts.

Plans not covered by ERISA, including IRAs and some 403(b) plans, have weaker protection. In bankruptcy, the Bankruptcy Abuse Prevention and Consumer Protection Act (BAPCPA) gives federal protection to IRAs up to about $1.4 million (with stronger protection for qualified plan rollovers and weaker protection for inherited IRAs). Outside of bankruptcy, state laws determine whether the assets are protected from creditors.

Extensive Example

Nora is 40 years old and has an income of $70,000, an employment income tax rate of 25 percent, a capital gains tax rate of 15 percent (assuming that the capital gains are long-term), and a dividend tax rate of 15 percent (assuming that the dividends are qualified). She has expenses (after-tax) of about $48,000, which makes up $48,000/(1 − 25%) = $64,000 of her pretax income. Thus, she believes that she can put aside $70,000 − $64,000 = $6,000 of pretax dollars to invest, and she is considering investing in a regular brokerage account, a traditional IRA, or a Roth IRA.

Which account type should Nora choose? In answering that question, I will, at least initially, assume that (i) she intends to invest in a stock portfolio with no dividends that is expected to give an annual return of 8 percent, (ii) she will leave the money intact for 30 years, at which point she will withdraw it all, and (iii) her tax rates remain the same over time. Furthermore, I will ignore other investments she might have or make in the future.

Regular Account

Figure 5.14 shows that the pretax income of $6,000 grows to a value after taxes of $39,165 after 30 years. Employment income taxes are levied in the year that the $6,000 of employment income is made, while investment income taxes are levied in the year that the stock portfolio is sold.

You might say that this is not completely realistic. On the one hand, you might argue that the true value should be higher because the stock

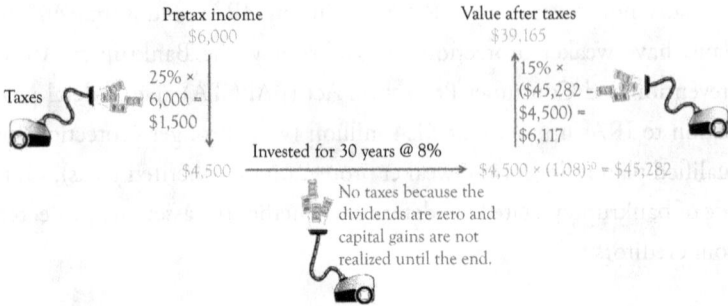

Figure 5.14 Example of investing in a regular brokerage account

portfolio permits loss harvesting that she otherwise could not make, and Nora might be more strategic in how she sells the stock (by not selling the stocks with the greatest capital gains). On the other hand, you might argue that the true value should be lower because most stock portfolios generate some dividends over time, such that taxes are paid in earlier years. Either way, the general conclusions and lessons of the example will not change.

Traditional IRA

Figure 5.15 shows that the pretax income of $6,000 grows to a value after taxes of $45,282 after 30 years. Employment income taxes are not levied in the year that the $6,000 of employment income is made; rather employment income taxes are levied in the year that the investment is withdrawn. The higher value here compared to the regular account stems entirely from the absence of investment income taxes.

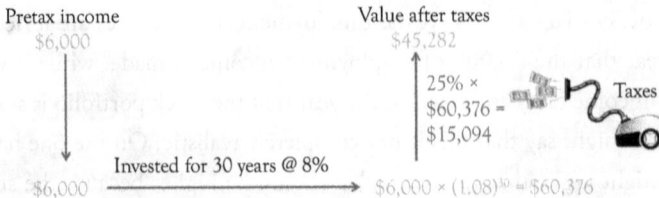

Figure 5.15 Example of investing in a traditional IRA

Roth IRA

Figure 5.16 shows that the pretax income of $6,000 grows to a value after taxes of $45,282 after 30 years. Employment income taxes are levied in the year that the $6,000 of employment income is made, and then there are no more taxes. The resulting value is identical to that for the traditional IRA because the employment income tax is assumed not to change over time.

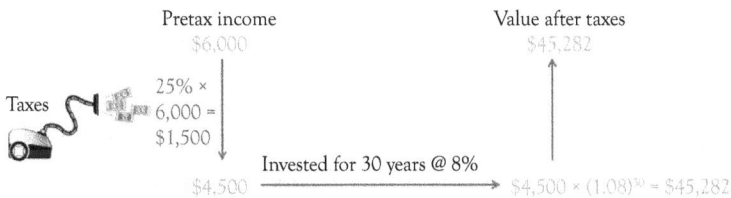

Figure 5.16 Example of investing in a Roth IRA

What If the Employment Income Tax Rate Drops?

What if Nora's employment income tax rate is expected to drop to 20 percent in 30 years because her income level is lower during retirement? The only account that changes value is the traditional IRA because the future withdrawals are taxed at the employment income tax rate. In particular, the after-tax value increases to $60,376 × (1 – 20%) = $48,301. Thus, with a falling employment income tax rate, the traditional IRA is better than the Roth IRA. The opposite would obviously also be true, that is, with an increasing employment income tax rate, the Roth IRA is better than the traditional IRA.

What If the Pretax Dollars Available to Invest Is Higher?

What would happen to the values in the IRAs if the pretax dollars available to invest is $8,000 instead of $6,000? Based on current regulations, Nora faces a contribution limit of $6,500 to her IRAs. With the $6,000 pretax contributed, she is close to that limit for the traditional IRA. But with the $6,000 pretax, she only contributes $6,000 × (1 – 25%) = $4,500 after tax to the Roth IRA, meaning that she is well within the limit. In fact, she could contribute the entire pretax income of $8,000, which would give an after-tax contribution to the Roth IRA of $8,000 × (1 − 25%) = $6,000.

If we change the $6,000 pretax income to $8,000 in the Roth IRA scenario and crunch the numbers again, we end up with an after-tax value of **$60,376** after 30 years.

The traditional IRA is a bit trickier. She can place maximum $6,500 in the IRA for an after-tax value of **$49,055** after 30 years (check this for yourself). She can place the remainder $1,500 in a regular account for an after-tax value of **$9,791** after 30 years (again, you can check this for yourself). Adding the two account values gives $49,055 + $9,791 = **$58,846**.

Comparing the two values shows that the Roth IRA is the better alternative here. The reason for this is that the Roth IRA essentially allows Nora to shield a larger portion of her pretax income from investment income taxes on subsequent investments. This is one of the benefits I mentioned earlier of Roth IRAs, but it is only relevant if you bump into the contribution limits on your IRAs. I think of the use of a Roth IRA for this purpose as expanding the maximum contribution to the IRAs.

What If Nora Invests in Dividend Stocks and Bonds?

What if Nora invests in stocks with dividend and bonds and not only zero-dividend stocks? Only one of the accounts would be affected then, namely the regular brokerage account, because IRAs evade taxes on investment income. The investment income in the regular brokerage account would be taxed in earlier years and not only when the capital gains are realized. As a result, the money that Nora pays to the IRS can no longer be used to generate more investment income, and the total value of the regular brokerage would be even lower relative to the IRAs.

What If Nora Will Travel the World Next Year?

What if Nora will travel the world next year, during which she will pay no income taxes? In that case, she should transfer the funds from her traditional IRA to a Roth IRA, and she will be able to bypass taxes altogether.

That is, the tax on the transfer is zero because her tax rate is zero, and the tax on withdrawals in 30 years is zero because it is a Roth IRA by then.[15] Thus, the after-tax value at the end is an astounding $60,376. This shows that if you think you will take a year off in the future, you should contribute funds to traditional IRAs now that you can transfer to a Roth IRA later.

Concept Tests

First Job After College

Grace, age 25, just got her first job after graduate school, as Figure 5.17 illustrates. The job has a salary of $55,000 and comes with annual contributions of $5,500 to a 401(k) plan. Can and should she open an IRA? If so, what kind of account and how much should she contribute?

Grace can contribute $6,500 to either a traditional IRA or a Roth IRA, and she should max out if she can. I would recommend a Roth IRA because her income tax rate is fairly low, and a Roth IRA has other benefits, including the ability to shield a greater portion of her pretax

Figure 5.17 Grace's calendar

---

[15] This assumes that the value of the transfer is less than the standard deduction ($13,850 for single filers in 2023)—which most likely will be the case here—so that Nora does not pay any taxes. Larger transfers might push the taxable income into a higher tax bracket.

income, the lack of RMD, and the lack of penalty for early withdrawal of the original contribution.

Student With Part-Time Job

Your daughter Emma is a college student who works part-time as a waitress, as Figure 5.18 illustrates, making $10,000 per year. The restaurant offers no retirement plan. Can and should she open an IRA? If so, what kind of account and how much should she contribute?

Because she does not pay any taxes (she is in the 10 percent income tax rate bracket, but the standard deduction exceeds her income), she should definitely open a Roth IRA and contribute the maximum of $6,500 (which is the minimum of $6,500 and her annual income). And if she cannot, you should help her do that. This is truly one of the golden opportunities out there in the wealth management world, and you can help your daughter get a superb start on her absolutely tax-free retirement savings.

Note that even minors with income from, say, mowing lawns can contribute toward a Roth IRA, but then their parents must help them open a custodial IRA, and the parents control the assets until the minors have reached the age of majority (i.e., 18 years old).

Figure 5.18 Emma in her job as waitress

Temporarily Unemployed

Joe just lost his bank job with an annual income of $85,000 during a severe industry downturn, as Figure 5.19 illustrates. He has accumulated investments of about $250,000 in a brokerage account, which should cover him during his job search. He also has a traditional IRA with about $150,000. Do you have any suggestions for how he might reshuffle his accounts?

It depends on the length of the job search. Assuming that it takes a prolonged period, his annual income likely falls substantially. If so, he should consider transferring funds from his traditional IRA to a Roth IRA while his employment income tax rate is low. However, he might not want to transfer the entire amount because that would push him into a higher tax bracket.

Some might argue that Joe should also harvest some capital gains by selling some securities with large accumulated capital gains in the regular brokerage account. But that does not work in conjunction with the transfer of funds from the traditional IRA to a Roth IRA because the transfer raises his tax rate. Thus, if Joe needs to sell some securities, he should probably sell those with a small capital gain.

Figure 5.19 Joe as unemployed

Potentially Broke

Brody, age 30, has $5,000 to invest in a traditional IRA, Roth IRA, or regular brokerage account. But he is concerned that he will run low on cash (and bank deposits) in a couple of years, as Figure 5.20 illustrates, because of unexpected expenses, for example, he might need to replace his old car. Thus, he would like to have access to the investment. What should he do?

Brody could certainly deposit some of the money in a bank account, but that would not generate much of a return. I would instead recommend that Brody contribute the money to a Roth IRA because it would allow him to withdraw the original contribution with no penalty, and the investment would grow tax-free. I would further recommend that he initially invest in some reasonably safe bonds and shift to stocks when it becomes clear that he will not need to withdraw the money in the short run. Note that the unexpected expenses are unlikely to qualify as financial hardship, so if Brody contributes the money to a traditional IRA, he would face a 10 percent penalty on withdrawals.

Figure 5.20 Brody's fear of being broke

Planning a Sabbatical Year

Sabina is a young professor of archeology with an annual income of $68,000. In five years, she is planning on taking a sabbatical year with no income, as Figure 5.21 illustrates. She has a 403(b) from her

Figure 5.21 Sabina on sabbatical

employer, and she is now considering also contributing toward a traditional IRA or a Roth IRA, both of which she qualifies for. What would you recommend?

Assuming that Sabina's annual income and employment income tax rate drop substantially during her sabbatical year, she should contribute pretax income to a traditional IRA over the next several years. With annual contributions of $6,500, she will have contributed $6,500 × 5 = $32,500 after five years, and the total value might be $50,000 with some decent returns. Then she should plan to transfer the funds from the traditional IRA to a Roth IRA during her sabbatical year when her employment income tax rate is low. One last thing: during her sabbatical year, she should contribute directly to the Roth IRA; while she could still take the detour via a traditional IRA that year, it is not necessary to do so.

Leaving Employment

Leah, age 35, just quit her job for another, as Figure 5.22 illustrates. Now she is contemplating what to do with her 401(k) from her former employment. Here are her choices for what to do with her old 401(k):

- Leave it alone.
- Liquidate it.

Figure 5.22 Leah leaving her job

- Move it to her new employment.
- Move it to an IRA.

What should she do?

By far the worst choice is to liquidate it. I would recommend Leah to move it to an IRA for several reasons. First, the IRA has more investment choices. Second, once the funds have been moved, she no longer must deal with the old HR department and/or plan administrator. Third, it is easier to manage an IRA. For example, if she has several IRAs, she can pool them for the purposes of satisfying the RMD requirements and only withdraw from one of them. Fourth, 401(k) plans often charge administration fees.

The simplest and safest way for Leah to move the funds from the old retirement account to an IRA is via a *trustee-to-trustee transfer*. This entails instructing the old plan administrator to transfer the funds directly to the IRA custodian and completing/signing some forms. The risky alternative is to withdraw the money from the 401(k) and redeposit it to an IRA within 60 days. But if you miss the deadline, you face a triple whammy: the withdrawal becomes taxable, you might have to pay an early-distribution penalty, and you cannot deposit the money back to a retirement account anymore. Another pitfall is that you are only allowed one such 60-day rollover per year to prevent people from abusing the system by frequently taking out "60-day IRA loans." Lastly, beware of any excessive fees for rolling over the funds to an IRA.

Incidentally, my advice would be the same for Leah if she were to leave the workforce for good, for example, to retire.

Asset Location: Roth IRA Versus Regular Brokerage Account

Let us try to combine some concepts from the last two chapters.

Sam recently heard the common recommendation of placing fixed-income securities in tax-advantaged accounts and stocks in regular brokerage accounts. Do you agree with this recommendation?

As argued in the last chapter, there are two determinants of asset location: (i) the level of invest income (securities with high invest income should be placed in tax-advantaged accounts) and (ii) the level of taxation (securities that are taxed more heavily should be placed in tax-advantaged accounts). The common asset location recommendation focuses on the second determinant. Fixed-income securities are indeed taxed heavily, which should place them in tax-advantaged accounts. But they also have lower investment income than stocks. Thus, it is unclear whether fixed-income securities belong to tax-advantaged or regular accounts.

Suppose that Sam will invest $12,000 (after tax), half in nondividend stocks with an expected return of 9 percent and the other half in bonds paying a yearly interest of 6 percent (and having zero expected capital gain). Sam can place a maximum of $6,500 in his Roth IRA (as of 2023) and the rest in a regular brokerage account, and he intends to withdraw the money after 30 years. His income tax rate (now and in the future) is 25 percent, dividend tax rate is 15 percent, and capital gains tax rate is 15 percent. Let us assume for simplicity that he will either place (i) all the stocks in the Roth IRA and all the bonds in a regular account, or (ii) all the stocks in a regular account and all the bonds in the Roth IRA. Which is the better alternative?

Alternative (i): If Sam places the stocks in a Roth IRA and the bonds in a regular account, he expects to have the following when he has withdrawn the funds in 30 years:

- Stocks: $6,000 \times 1.09^{30} = \$79,606$
- Bonds: $6,000 \times 1.045^{30} = \$22,472$ (the 4.5 percent is 6 percent less the tax on interest of $25\% \times 6\% = 1.5\%$)
- Total $= \$79,606 + \$22,472 = \$102,078$

Alternative (ii): If he places the stocks in a regular account and the bonds in a Roth IRA, he expects to have the following when he has withdrawn the funds in 30 years:

- Stocks: $6,000 \times 1.09^{30} = \$79,606$, less capital gains tax $= 15\% \times (\$79,606 - \$6,000) = \$11,041$
- Bonds: $6,000 \times 1.06^{30} = \$34,461$
- Total $= \$79,606 - \$11,041 + \$34,461 = \$103,026$

This shows that he should place the bonds in a Roth IRA, consistent with the common recommendation.

What if the expected return on stocks is 10 percent instead? In that case, the expected stock portfolio after 30 years is $104,696, and the capital gains tax when withdrawn from a regular account is $14,804. That means that the total value if Sam places the bonds in a regular account ($104,696 + $22,472 = $127,168), is now higher than if he places the bonds in a Roth IRA ($104,696 − $14,804 + $34,461 = $124,353).

What if the expected return on stocks is 9 percent, but 2 percent of it is dividend yield? The calculations are then more complex, and you can try them yourself. It turns out that it is better to keep the bonds in a regular account (the total value is $102,078) than in a Roth IRA (the total value is $99,629, dragged down by the earlier taxation of the dividends in the regular account).

Lastly, what if Sam expects to leave the accounts to his heirs? Assuming that the step-up in basis is still in place, the capital gains tax essentially disappears from the calculations above, and it consistently makes sense to keep the bonds in the Roth IRA and the stocks in the regular account (where they no longer face capital gains taxes).

CHAPTER 6

Protecting Your Wealth

Most individuals are averse to risk, at least downside risk. But not all downside risks truly matter. If you drop your iPhone on the concrete pavement and the screen cracks, you will obviously get upset. Yet the incident probably does not have a real consequence for your financial health. In contrast, if the stock market collapses, your investment might take a hit that forces you to change your life, for example, by delaying retirement or constraining leisure activities. Some individuals might even lose their jobs and spiral into credit card debt and payday loans, leading to chronic poverty.

In some cases, we can readily and cheaply reduce the downside risk to our financial health. But in other cases, reducing risk is unnecessary, challenging, or simply too expensive.

The main objectives for this chapter are:

- Explore some of the ways individuals can reduce risk and the net benefit of doing so to financial wealth.
- Learn what risks individuals should manage, for example, via insurance, and what risks to disregard.

Insurance (and Warranties)

Insurance contracts, as illustrated in Figure 6.1, protect against prespecified financial losses. For example, car insurance protects against financial losses from a car crash, while house insurance protects against financial losses from a fire, though it can obviously never recover items of nostalgia. The insurance contracts can be entered into with (or "bought from") a variety of insurance companies, even though these companies never had anything to do with, for example, the manufacturing of the car or the building of the house to be insured.

Figure 6.1 Insurance

Warranties are guarantees from the manufacturer promising to make repairs or replacements under certain conditions and within a specified period, and they come as part of the purchase. For example, a car manufacturer might promise to repair or replace faulty components for three years or 36,000 miles after the purchase, whichever comes first. Because you typically do not have much say regarding such warranties, I will not discuss them further. Third parties might also sell so-called extended warranties, but these are really just service contracts. Because their terms and conditions are generally bad compared to their prices, extended warranties are typically rip-offs, and you should almost always avoid them. Enough said about warranties and service contracts, then, though you might find that a lot of the discussion below on insurance also pertains to warranties and service contracts.

Problems With Insurance

Insurance is a good idea in theory in that individuals reduce the risk of financial losses, while insurance companies take on the risk but diversify it across many customers. But the world of insurance is filled with information, measurement, and behavioral problems. When such problems are severe, the prices of insurance (i.e., the insurance premiums) increase, making insurance less appealing for individuals to buy. It is useful to recognize when insurance works well and when it suffers from problems, as summarized in Table 6.1, because it helps us make better insurance decisions. I have been told, though, that this subsection is a bit scholarly, and I won't be offended if you skip ahead to the next subsection on general guidelines.

Insurance works well when there are many fairly homogenous exposure units, such as buildings or cars. This facilitates the estimation of future losses based on historical data and, thereby, the pricing of the insurance. In addition, it allows the insurance company to diversify its risk across units. If, conversely, you wish to insure a Picasso painting, there is little data on which to estimate possible losses, and it is challenging for the insurance company to diversify its exposure. Thus, the insurance company might be unwilling to insure the painting, or if it does, it will charge a premium that far exceeds what is actuarially fair.[1]

Second, insurance works well when any loss is clear and measurable. Such losses make it quick and easy for the insurance company to make the

Table 6.1 *When insurance works well or poorly*

Insurance works well	Insurance works poorly
Homogenous exposure units	Heterogeneous exposure units
Losses are clear and measurable	Losses are unclear and difficult to measure
Information is transparent	The insured and insurer have access to different information, giving rise to *adverse selection*
Losses are accidental and beyond the control of the insured	The behavior of the insured affects the losses, giving rise to *moral hazard*

---

[1] Actuarially fair means that the premium equals the expected value of the loss. For example, if there is a 5 percent probability of a one million dollar loss over the next year, the actuarially fair premium is $1,000,000 × 5% = $50,000.

payouts. Conversely, ambiguous losses might give rise to costly disagreements and even fraud.

Third, insurance works well when the insurer and the insured have access to the same information about the exposure units. This minimizes *adverse selection*, in which individuals only insure exposure units that are most likely to produce a large insurance payoff. This problem is especially severe for health insurance, where individuals with pre-existing conditions or unhealthy/dangerous habits are more inclined to purchase health insurance than other individuals. An example is a skateboarder who recognizes his large chance of injury and, thus, the need for health insurance that covers any treatment costs. The consequence of such adverse selection is that insurance premiums soar and only the riskiest assets/individuals are insured, or, in the worst case, the insurance market collapses. One way to reduce adverse selection is for the insurance company to gather more information. However, customers might hide their high risk, like the skateboarder in Figure 6.2. Furthermore, information gathering is costly, and the costs are ultimately borne by all insured customers via higher premiums.

Fourth, insurance works well when any loss is accidental and beyond the control of the insured. This minimizes *moral hazard*, in which the insured inflates the risk at the expense of the insurance company. An

Figure 6.2 Adverse selection

Figure 6.3 Moral hazard

example of moral hazard is the skateboarder with health insurance in Figure 6.3, who deliberately takes greater risk knowing that any self-imposed injuries are covered. Another example is that people with comprehensive car insurance are likely to drive and behave more recklessly, for example, by exceeding speed limits and leaving the car out in hailstorms, because they believe that their actions have limited downsides. Faced with great moral hazard, the insurance company could try to monitor and change behavior by placing tracking devices in the car, perhaps in exchange for lower premiums. But such tracking devices can be costly and present privacy concerns.

General Guidelines

Some insurance is required. For example, just about all states require a minimum level of car insurance by law, including liability insurance that covers bodily injury to other people and damage to other people's property. Furthermore, mortgage lenders require home insurance. Beyond this, you are generally free to choose your level of insurance. So, what should you choose?

You should first ask yourself what the worst-case scenario would be for your financial health in the absence of insurance. The reason is that you only need to insure against events that would be devastating to your financial health. Why, you might ask, should you not always buy insurance to be on the safe side? The simple reason is that insurance premiums are not actuarially fair because the insurance company expects the premium paid to exceed the expected value of the compensation. This is especially so when the insurance products are riddled with adverse selection, moral hazard, and the other problems listed earlier, because the insurance company then also wants the premium to cover additional screening/monitoring costs and compensation for additional risk.[2]

If you believe that you need insurance, you should carry the largest deductible you can afford. The downside is that it effectively reduces your insurance coverage. The upside is that it also reduces the inherent conflict between you and the insurance company, thereby reducing adverse selection and moral hazard problems. In return, you should get a premium that is more actuarially fair.

You might also consider self-insurance in place of commercial insurance. That is, you could set aside the money that you ordinarily would have paid as an insurance premium (and perhaps more in the beginning) in a rainy-day account to cover potential future losses. Naturally, this only works if the potential losses are moderate. For potential losses that could ruin you, you should get commercial insurance.

Oh, one last thing: my advice for health insurance differs notably, and I discuss that more next.

Health Insurance

While I am lukewarm about most voluntary insurance, I strongly advocate health insurance in a system without nationalized health care. There are four reasons for this.[3]

---

[2] An exception might be in the case of adverse selection where *you* hold the information advantage. For example, you might know that the risk of a flood in your neighborhood is higher than what the insurance company assumes when setting the flood insurance premium, in which case it makes sense to buy flood insurance.

[3] Note that some young people who are over 65 or have disabilities might qualify for Medicare, which is a federal health insurance program.

First, getting seriously sick in the absence of health insurance could give rise to exorbitant expenses that put you in financial ruin. In that sense, the case of health insurance meets the general criterion for when to get insurance discussed in the previous subsection.

Second, health insurance is unique in that the insurance providers not only cover the health care expenses but also negotiate lower prices with the health care providers. If you are uninsured and must pay for the services yourself, you must pay a considerably higher price, perhaps even several times higher!

Third, employer-sponsored health care insurance is essentially untaxed compensation and, thus, a particularly good deal. Thus, you should seek out an employer that provides health care insurance, even if that means a slightly lower salary.

Fourth, uninsured individuals often fail to seek medical care when they are sick. This means that, for example, the chance to discover early stages of cancer is diminished. Even preventative care is likely to suffer in the absence of insurance.[4]

Disability Insurance

Perhaps your most valuable asset is your future income stream from employment. If you cannot work because of illness or disability, you will lose that asset. The probability that a 35-year-old becomes disabled before the age of 65 is as high as 20 percent. For most individuals, this would be a serious financial setback. Thus, based on our general criterion for when to get insurance, disability insurance, which replaces your income in the short- or long-term, is sensible. Fortunately, most employers provide some kind of disability insurance or offer it as a voluntary benefit, and you might even be able to get additional disability insurance through your employer. In any event, you can purchase a private policy.

---

[4] You might argue that people without insurance have an incentive to take better care of their health. Unfortunately, I believe that most individuals who disregard health insurance also disregard their health until it fails or they cannot afford to invest in it.

Long-Term Care Insurance

Most individuals will, at some point, need assistance with their activities of daily living (ADLs), including bathing, dressing, and toileting. The cost of such assistance can range from less than $50,000 per year for in-home care to more than $100,000 per year for nursing home care, which can be a substantial financial setback, especially for those who need it for several years.

Long-term care insurance is designed to cover the costs of assistance not covered by regular health insurance. In a typical case, an individual would start buying long-term care insurance at age 60 and pay $2,000 to $3,000 per year for benefits of $165,000 that grow 2 percent annually (but would have a daily limit). Women need longer care on average and pay a higher premium than men.

For those who might be unable to pay for long-term care, long-term care insurance could be a reasonable option. But it is quite expensive relative to expected benefits, so it should not be viewed as an investment. Furthermore, it comes with many restrictions and conditions, so it can be hard to get reimbursements for the actual costs of care.

Life Insurance

Life insurance provides financial support to dependents in the event of a loss of income from death. Pure death insurance that only pays upon death is called *term life* and is illustrated in Figure 6.4. Term life insurance provides protection for a specific period ("term") like 10 to 20 years, and can be renewed thereafter. It is sometimes offered via the workplace as so-called group term life insurance.

Not everyone needs life insurance, and your needs vary across your lifespan. If you have no dependents, there is no need for life insurance. Thus, many individuals might need life insurance when they have young children, but as their children grow up and become self-sufficient, the need for life insurance gradually diminishes. By the age of 60, few individuals need life insurance anymore.

You also do not need life insurance if you have a substantial estate, even if you have dependents. In that case, you will obviously no longer need the estate for personal consumption if you die, and it can be fully used to take care of your dependents.

Figure 6.4 Term life insurance

For those who need life insurance, the question is how large the coverage should be. That is, how much *death benefit* (i.e., what gets paid upon death) is needed? A common rule of thumb is to get life insurance with a death benefit that is 10 times your annual income. There are a few reasons why this is likely to be sufficient:

- Unlike employment income, the death benefit is not taxable. (An exception is that any interest received due to postponed death payments is taxable as interest income.)
- If the death benefit is paid out as a lump sum (which is most common), the money can be invested and generate investment income until it is needed. The death benefit could alternatively be converted to an annuity, which would also come with built-in investment income.
- Many household expenses decrease substantially when a breadwinner passes, though this might be offset by, for example, increased child care expenses.

Suppose that you get married in your mid-20s and have a couple of children in the years thereafter. Then your need for life insurance might be roughly as depicted in Figure 6.5, which might peak at, say, 12 times your salary of $85K.

To meet that life insurance need, you could acquire a 20-year term life insurance policy shortly before the first child is born and a 10-year term life insurance policy shortly before the second child is born, both with a death benefit of $500K. Figure 6.6 depicts this ladder strategy.

Fortunately, term life insurance premiums are reasonable when you are young and healthy. If you are 30 years old and in great health, you can purchase term life insurance with a death benefit of $500,000 for a few hundred dollars per year, as Figure 6.7 shows (with data from policygenius.com).

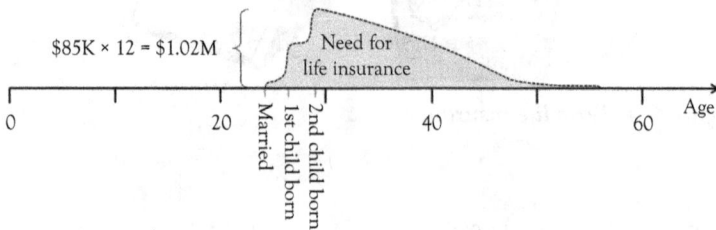

Figure 6.5 The need for life insurance

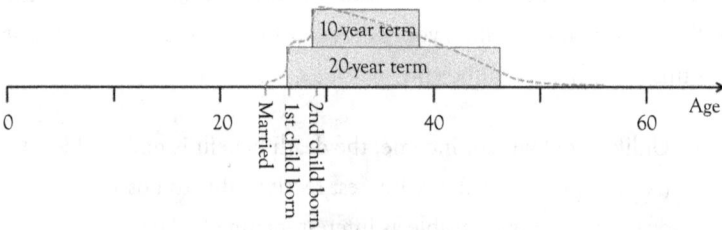

Figure 6.6 Ladder strategy for life insurance need

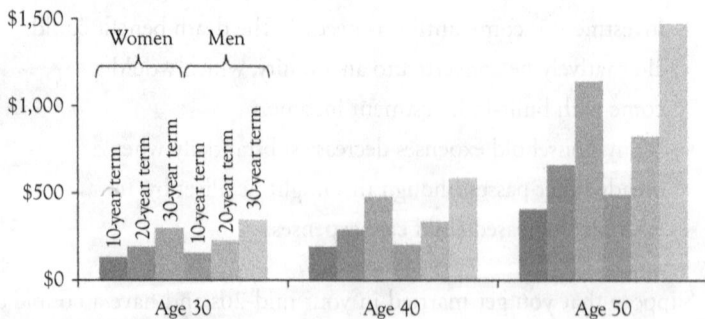

Figure 6.7 Annual premiums for term life with best health and death benefit of $500,000

Note that you can also buy a life insurance policy on someone else, given that (a) you have an "insurable interest" in the person covered by the policy and (b) the person covered by the policy consents. Insurable interest means that you experience an emotional or financial loss when the insured person dies, for example, if the insured person is a family member or business partner. Furthermore, you can transfer ownership of a life insurance policy to another adult, including the policy beneficiary, by filling out some paperwork from the issuing company. If the transfer occurs at least three years before death, it will not be included in the estate of the deceased.

If you start discussing life insurance with an insurance salesperson, it is likely that she will also try to sell you some pricey investment/savings product as part of the insurance contract because that earns her a hefty commission. In that case, we are talking about *permanent life insurance*, which you can think of as death insurance plus a savings plan, where the savings plan makes up the larger component, at least in terms of cost to you. I will postpone a more complete discussion of permanent life insurance until the chapter on alternative investments because the savings product of the contract really has nothing to do with traditional insurance.

Protecting Your Stock Portfolio

When you first start investing, you should assess how much risk you can take. If you are able to take more risk in pursuit of a higher return, you should invest mostly in stocks, while if you are unable to take much risk, you should invest mostly in fixed-income securities. Recall, however, that if you have an investment horizon of 15 years or more, you are almost always better off placing your money in a diversified stock portfolio than in safer fixed-income securities. The reason for this is twofold: (i) the return is exponentially increasing over time, making the higher return for stocks more dominant over longer horizons; and (ii) the risk increases at a decreasing rate over time.

Once you have chosen your investments, you really should not have to make any significant adjustments. Rather, you should stay the course and stay calm. By doing that, you should hopefully accumulate a portfolio over time that is so valuable and resilient that you can endure even serious market downturns.

Figure 6.8 Adjusting portfolio risk

Nevertheless, situations might arise that call for you to dial down the risk in your portfolio, as Figure 6.8 illustrates. For example, you might encounter some large and unexpected expenses that put a severe dent in your financial health. Or individuals with a more modest portfolio value might need to reduce risk as they approach retirement and their investment horizon shortens. In that case, what can you do?

Change Future Contributions

If you have a retirement account, you can readily change future contributions toward less risky securities, like Treasury securities. However, the effect of this strategy will not be evident for quite some time, as the existing portfolio composition does not change. Thus, you might need some more drastic measures.

Sell a Portion of Stock Portfolio

You could sell off a portion of your stock portfolio and invest the proceeds in less risky securities. Depending on the portion that you sell, this reallocation could have a dramatic effect on the riskiness of your investments. But it will, of course, also reduce your expected future return.

Pursuing a reallocation is a relatively pain-free maneuver in a retirement account. But it could trigger large tax liabilities in a regular brokerage account. Thus, if you intend to sell off a large portion of your stocks in your regular brokerage account, you should tread carefully by selling a set of stocks that net out to have minimal capital gains, like I discussed in an earlier chapter.

Note also that most retirement plans offer *target-date funds*, which essentially automate the process of dialing down the risk of your retirement portfolio as you age by reallocating the assets. A later chapter discusses such funds in greater detail.

Use Stock Options

In recent years, stock options have become popular among some amateurs. I personally dislike this development. Most amateurs use options for speculative purposes, which is treacherous because of their wild valuation fluctuations. In addition, options trading comes with high transaction costs. Lastly, options trading requires your complete attention as option expiration approaches to make sure that you sell or exercise whatever options you have that are *in-the-money*. Thus, I recommend that you leave options to the professionals.

However, if you have a strong need to reduce portfolio risk and cannot reallocate without facing a stiff tax bill, it would be feasible to use put options to meet your need. Put options give the holder the right, but not the obligation, to sell individual stocks or a stock index at a prespecified price called the exercise price. Thus, if you also hold the underlying stock or index, you are essentially insured against prices falling below the exercise price. Note, however, that most options have a fairly short maturity, so you must keep buying them at regular intervals to remain insured.

Buy Inverse ETFs

An exchange-traded fund (ETF) on, say, the S&P 500 index is a fund of securities that is designed to track the performance of the S&P 500 index. An *inverse* ETF on, say, the S&P 500 index is a fund of securities that is designed to move in the opposite direction of the S&P 500 index, at least on a day-to-day basis. You can even purchase leveraged inverse ETFs that magnify the effect, such as one with the ticker symbol SPXU. Thus, if the S&P 500 index drops 2 percent one day, a standard inverse ETF on the index will increase by 2 percent the same day, while a 3× inverse

ETF would increase by 6 percent. That also implies that inverse ETFs are expected to have a negative return. (Just search online for "SPXU" to see its historical performance.)

You can therefore purchase inverse ETFs to offset the risk in an existing portfolio. A benefit over stock options is that inverse ETFs do not expire. But the fees are a bit high, perhaps as much as 1 percent on an annualized basis. Also, an inverse ETF is only effective in reducing your portfolio risk if your portfolio resembles the index that the ETF is designed to move against. Thus, a better solution in the long run is to reallocate your portfolio if this can be done without incurring a large tax bill.

Example of Protecting a Stock Portfolio in a Pandemic

Corey and Pamela have a stock portfolio worth $80,000 that closely resembles the S&P 500. At the beginning of February 2020, they fear that the looming COVID-19 will wreak havoc on the value of their investment. Thus, they are considering moving their investment from stocks to bonds. Alternatively, they could sell $20,000 of stock to buy SPXU, a triple-inverse ETF. With stock worth $60,000 (or 75 percent of the total value) and triple inverse ETFs worth $20,000 (25 percent), the ETFs are worth one-third of the stock. But the ETF value is designed to move three times as much and in a different direction, so the combination of the stock portfolio and the triple inverse ETF should be fairly immune to market fluctuations.

The graphs in Figure 6.9 show the value of their portfolio over the next couple of months if they were to hold on to the stocks, shift to

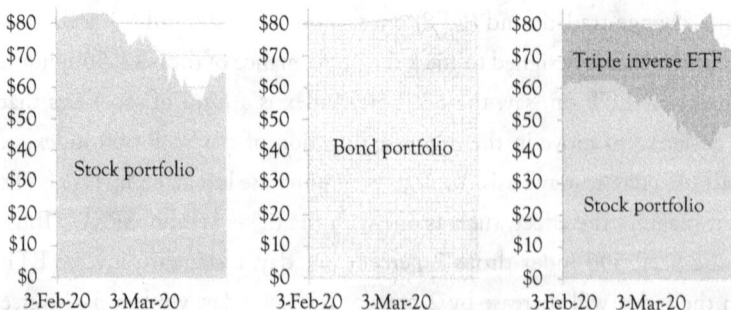

Figure 6.9 Porfolio values during the pandemic

bonds, or buy some triple inverse ETFs. If they were to hold on to the stock, the value of their investment would drop dramatically from $80K to a low of $55K and then increase again to about $65K. The bond portfolio also exhibits some fluctuations, but they are modest compared to those of the stock portfolio. As designed, the combination of the stock and the inverse ETFs stays very stable at first because any changes in the value of the stock portfolio are offset almost perfectly by opposite changes in the value of the inverse ETF. But the hedge does not work as well after large changes in the market value. Essentially, the stock portfolio, which initially was worth three times as much as the ETFs, is slipping in value relative to the ETFs so that the movements in the ETF start to dominate the total portfolio value.[5]

Overall, in this example of a collapse in the stock market, both the shift to bonds and a partial shift to inverse ETFs would have offered protection. The bond strategy worked the best but would also require the whole stock portfolio to be liquidated, perhaps triggering a large capital gains tax if the money is in a regular brokerage account.

---

[5] This hedge could have been improved by selling some of the ETFs to buy stock after market declines and vice versa.

CHAPTER 7

More on Funds

Most individuals prefer the convenience of investing in funds to purchasing the underlying securities to attain diversification in their investments. Given this preference, we should understand what fund types are available and their suitability for individual investors.

The main objectives for this chapter are:

- Learn the characteristics of various types of funds, including their investment choices, fees, and tax efficiency.
- Develop an understanding for what types of funds are most suitable for individual investors.

Mutual Funds

Mutual funds pool money from investors and purchase stocks, bonds, and other assets. Mutual fund investors own a slice of the fund's portfolio and participate proportionally in any of the fund's gains or losses. Investors who buy shares in a mutual fund send cash to the fund company, and those who want to redeem their shares return the shares to the fund company in exchange for cash.

The price of a share in a mutual fund is referred to as the net asset value (NAV) per share, and it is computed at the end of each trading day as the total value of the securities in the portfolio divided by the mutual fund shares outstanding. Thus, if you order a mutual fund share during the trading day, you pay whatever the NAV per share is estimated to be at the end of the trading day.

Mutual funds can be either passively or actively managed. Passive funds track a market index, for example, the S&P 500 or a certain segment of the market. Conversely, actively managed funds spend substantial resources to identify undervalued securities to try to "beat the market," that is, outperform passive funds with similar risk profiles. While mutual funds' prospectuses describe their investment strategies, mutual funds must only disclose their holdings once every quarter (and then with a 30-day lag). Thus, there is often uncertainty regarding the composition of their portfolios, especially for actively managed funds.

Mutual funds have two types of fees:

- Annual operating fees (expense ratio): These fees cover the operating expenses of the funds and include management fees to pay fund managers, 12b-1 fees to cover marketing expenses and shareholder services, and other fees to cover miscellaneous expenses. They are expressed as a fraction of the investment value in the *expense ratio*. The expense ratio varies greatly across funds, from 0.015 percent for some passive index funds to more than 2 percent for some pricey actively managed funds.
- Shareholder fees: These fees stem from purchasing and selling mutual fund shares, especially in the case of broker-sold funds. A broker might charge commissions. Furthermore, mutual funds might charge front-end loads for purchases and back-end loads and/or redemption fees for sales, where the loads typically go to the broker, and the redemption fees go to the fund to cover its redemption costs.

Note that while operating expenses and load charges are explicitly disclosed in the fund prospectus, other costs (including other transaction costs and the price impact of the trades) are not. In general, you should avoid load funds (as there is no evidence that they perform better than no-load funds) and funds with high expense ratios, and you should keep mutual fund transactions to a minimum.

While investing in mutual funds is convenient, doing so can trigger substantially higher taxes than if investors were to directly hold the underlying securities in the funds. Thus, you should be wary of holding mutual funds, especially actively managed funds, in regular brokerage accounts. Let me elaborate.

Mutual funds, especially those that are actively managed, continuously rebalance their portfolios by selling securities to either accommodate shareholder redemptions or reallocate investments. Such sales trigger realized capital gains for the mutual fund investors, and these gains are normally distributed to the mutual fund investors in November or December.[1] Thus, even though the investors did not trade the mutual fund during the year, they must pay capital gains taxes on any capital gains distributions they received that year.[2] Whether the capital gain is deemed to be short-term or long-term depends on how long the mutual fund held the securities and not how long the investors have held the mutual fund.[3]

Exchange-Traded Funds

Here is what all investors should know about exchange-traded funds (ETFs) in one paragraph: Like mutual funds, ETFs pool money from individual investors to purchase portfolios of securities. But unlike mutual funds (and like individual stocks), ETFs are traded on stock exchanges, and ETF prices are continuously updated during trading hours. Most ETFs are passive index funds and, thus, tend to have low fees.[4] Indeed, their average expense ratio is only 0.2 percent. Investors might also have to pay commissions when trading ETFs, but these are modest, and ETFs do not charge loads.

---

[1] The website www.capgainsvalet.com provides estimates of capital gains distributions and a list of funds "in the doghouse."

[2] You could dodge that tax liability by selling the mutual fund prior to the year-end distribution. But in that case, you cannot repurchase the fund within 30 days to comply with the wash-sale rule.

[3] Similarly, whether any dividends that the mutual fund passes through to its investors are deemed to be qualified for tax purposes also depends on the holding period of the mutual fund.

[4] However, many exotic ETFs have entered the marketplace in recent years with high fees.

Are you willing to go a bit further? I do not want to get too technical here, but I will briefly discuss the creation/redemption mechanism of ETFs because it serves as the foundation for their competitive edge, including their tax efficiency.

Before ETF providers (e.g., BlackRock, Vanguard, and State Street) launch ETF shares, they establish a partnership with one or several authorized participants (APs), which are other financial institutions (e.g., Goldman Sachs and JP Morgan). The APs then acquire the underlying securities of the ETF, for example, all the securities in the S&P 500 for an ETF that tracks the S&P 500 index. The APs deliver those shares to the ETF provider in exchange for a block of equally valued ETF shares, say 50,000 shares, called a creation unit. Finally, the APs sell the ETF shares in the stock market, and investors start trading ETF shares among themselves. I should also note that most ETF providers disclose their portfolios of underlying securities daily, either by law in the case of actively managed ETFs or by custom in the case of index ETFs.

The prices of the ETF shares might deviate slightly from the value of the underlying securities because of excessive or lackluster demand for the ETF or market inefficiencies. If the ETF shares trade at a premium, the APs buy more of the underlying securities in the market to initiate the creation of more ETF shares. Conversely, if the ETF shares trade at a discount, the APs buy the ETF shares in the market and redeem them for the underlying securities, which the APs can sell in the market for a profit. Thus, the ETF prices remain close to the value of their underlying securities.

The creation and redemption process allows the ETF provider to avoid the use of cash, as its transactions with the APs involve swaps of shares with similar values. As such, a loophole in the tax code states that there are no realizations of capital gains, and the ETF provider does not have to distribute capital gains to the ETF investors.[5] That is great news for all of us who hold ETF shares in regular brokerage accounts because it defers our capital gains tax burden.

---

[5] Mutual funds rarely exploit this loophole in the tax code because their investors typically want cash upon redemption. An exception is Vanguard, which has developed a proprietary method to exploit the loophole for its mutual funds.

Hedge Funds

Like mutual funds, hedge funds pool capital from investors that the funds in turn invest. But while mutual funds are restricted in its investments, hedge funds invest in a wide array of assets (real estate, commodities, etc.), securities (primarily stocks and bonds), and derivatives (including options), going both long (e.g., buying a stock) and short (e.g., borrowing a stock that is then sold, with the promise to buy it back later and return it to the lender). In fact, the name "hedge" fund stems from the idea that hedge funds take long and short positions in a wide array of assets and securities, which, in theory, should "hedge" the portfolio, that is, reduce the risk of the portfolio. In practice, though, most hedge funds pursue aggressive and unconventional investments and often lever up the risk of investors' positions by taking up debt to invest even more.

Hedge funds are not required to disclose what they are holding, not even to their investors, and will rarely do so. This, combined with their investment flexibility, makes hedge funds a black box, as in Figure 7.1.

Are you not scared off yet? Well, hedge funds are only offered privately to *accredited*, that is, wealthy and supposedly sophisticated,

Figure 7.1 Hedge fund as a black box

investors.[6] The regulators presume that these hedge fund investors can take care of themselves and, therefore, subject hedge funds to limited oversight and afford them great operational flexibility. There is, however, a loophole for regular investors to indirectly invest in hedge funds—they can invest in *funds of funds* (FOFs), which means that they invest in mutual funds that, in turn, invest in hedge funds. In that case, the mutual funds act as so-called "feeder" funds for the hedge funds.[7]

Are you still interested in investing in hedge funds? Here are my final arguments to keep you away. First, it might be hard to withdraw your money invested in hedge funds without months or years of advance notice. Second, hedge funds charge hefty fees; the standard fee is 2 percent of the value and 20 percent of profits (commonly referred to as "2-and-20").[8] As a result, the empirical evidence shows that hedge fund investors are likely to get a considerably lower investment return than those who simply invest in index funds.

Comparison of Fund Types

It is useful to summarize some key differences between the fund types we have discussed. A couple of important differences relate to (i) investment strategies, ranging from passive index funds to funds that have no constraints in their search for *alpha*, that is, a superior investment return, and (ii) fees, ranging from close to zero to several percent of the investment value plus a cut of profits. The two characteristics tend to go hand-in-hand, which is why I only use one dimension in Figure 7.2. Beware, however, that funds with similar investment strategies, for example, tracking the S&P 500, can vary in their fees.

---

[6] The requirements to be an individual accredited investor include (a) a net worth above $1,000,000 or an annual income above $200,000 over the past few years and (b) a sound understanding of the financial markets and investing. Individual hedge funds might also require minimum investment levels (often $100,000 or more) and only accept specially selected investors.

[7] The many small investors who got burnt in the Madoff scandal had invested in Madoff's hedge fund via such feeder funds.

[8] Steven Cohen's hedge fund SAC Capital Advisors reportedly charged a whopping 3-and-50, meaning a 3 percent expense ratio plus a 50 percent cut of profits.

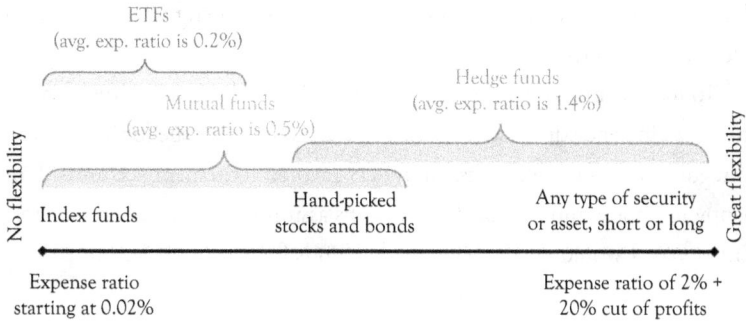

ETFs
(avg. exp. ratio is 0.2%)

Hedge funds
(avg. exp. ratio is 1.4%)

Mutual funds
(avg. exp. ratio is 0.5%)

No flexibility

Great flexibility

Index funds

Hand-picked
stocks and bonds

Any type of security
or asset, short or long

Expense ratio
starting at 0.02%

Expense ratio of 2% +
20% cut of profits

Figure 7.2 Fees and flexibility across fund types

The annual fees represented by the expense ratio are particularly harmful over time, slowly chipping away at your investment like termites damage a house. Figure 7.3 shows the value of a $1,000 investment with an annual return of 8 percent after 30 years for different fee levels. A modest expense ratio of 0.5 percent erodes 13 percent of your total investment value after 30 years, while a more aggressive expense ratio of 1.5 percent erodes more than one-third of the investment!

You might conclude that ETFs are preferable to mutual funds because of their lower fees. However, the lower average expense ratio for ETFs is misleading. The primary reason for the lower average expense ratio for ETFs is that a larger portion of them are index funds. In fact, if you compare fees for index ETFs and index mutual funds, you are likely to find

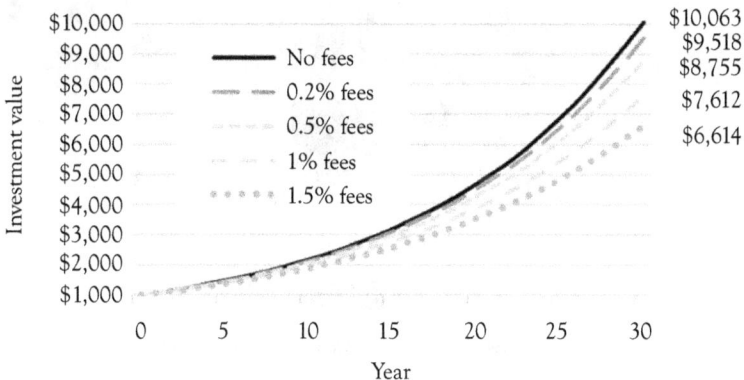

Investment value

$10,000
$9,000
$8,000
$7,000
$6,000
$5,000
$4,000
$3,000
$2,000
$1,000

—— No fees
⸺ ⸺ 0.2% fees
0.5% fees
1% fees
• • • • • 1.5% fees

$10,063
$9,518
$8,755
$7,612

$6,614

0   5   10   15   20   25   30

Year

Figure 7.3 The effect of annual fees

that the fees for the latter are lower. Thus, the main edge that ETFs have over mutual funds is not their fees.

To me, the primary advantage that ETFs have relative to mutual funds is their tax efficiency discussed earlier. But that is only an issue for investments in regular brokerage accounts. In my tax-favored retirement accounts, I am happy to choose mutual funds over ETFs assuming the fees are reasonable. Either way, I would never choose hedge funds for any of my accounts.

Concept Test—ETFs Versus Hedge Funds

Avery, as depicted in Figure 7.4, is very wealthy, yet very risk-averse. Although he is a so-called accredited investor who could invest in hedge funds, he has decided to bypass them in favor of ETFs. He simply views hedge funds to be too risky, especially after hearing of the Madoff debacle. Do you agree with Avery's assessment?

Avery is generally correct in his assessment of risk. Despite their names, hedge funds are typically more aggressive than mutual funds and

Figure 7.4 Avery, the wealthy and risk-averse investor

ETFs, which translates to high risk. But there is great variation in the risk level of hedge funds. Furthermore, there are many ETFs that are also very risky, including many of those that focus on narrow sectors or small countries or those that use leverage to boost performance. Thus, if Avery seeks to limit the volatility, he should pick an ETF with a broad portfolio and no leverage.

A bonus of Avery's choice is that he will likely receive a higher return than he would have received from a hedge fund because hedge funds tend to charge very high fees.

Ready-Made Funds

If you do not want to construct your own portfolios, many financial institutions (including Vanguard, Fidelity, and T. Rowe Price) conveniently provide ready-made funds (RMFs) that are likely to fit your needs. These funds are designed to match your investment horizon (target-date funds) and/or risk tolerance (target-risk funds).

RMFs rarely invest directly in individual stocks or bonds, but rather invest in an array of other funds, which technically makes them a type of FOF. The underlying funds typically come from the same institution. For example, an RMF from Vanguard consists of several different stock and bond funds that Vanguard offers separately.

The main drawback with RMFs is that expenses might incur at two levels: at the RMF fund level and the underlying funds level. This means that you should be extra careful to check fees before investing in RMFs. Fortunately, though, the expenses have fallen over time as various providers have been battling for market share, and some do not charge double fees anymore.

I would generally recommend reasonably finance-savvy individuals, including those who have reached this chapter, to avoid RMFs because of their fees and lack of flexibility. You can easily emulate their strategies on your own, and that way, you can obtain more tax flexibility, which is especially important for investments in regular brokerage accounts.

Target-Date Funds

Target-date funds, also known as lifecycle funds, are funds designed to fit certain investment horizons, or target dates. In most cases, the target date is the expected retirement date, but it could also be, say, the expected time of college admission in the case of college savings.

With long investment horizons, target-date funds contain lots of risk from large stock positions. As the investment horizons shorten, the funds gradually reduce the risk along a *glide path* by reallocating away from stocks and toward bonds, as Figure 7.5 depicts.

The Pension Protection Act of 2006 (PPA) was established to enhance workers' retirement security. PPA allows employers to make target-date funds the default option for employees' retirement plans, with the idea that this helps inattentive or financially unsophisticated employees with their retirement savings. Consequently, many employers, including the University of Iowa, made target-date funds the default choice. This naturally led to a dramatic increase in both the number of target-date funds and the total value of those funds to about $3 trillion in 2021.

Assuming that the fees of the target-date funds are reasonable, I believe that these funds are a good choice for financially unsophisticated employees and a good default for both financially unsophisticated and inattentive employees. A large chunk of those employees would otherwise

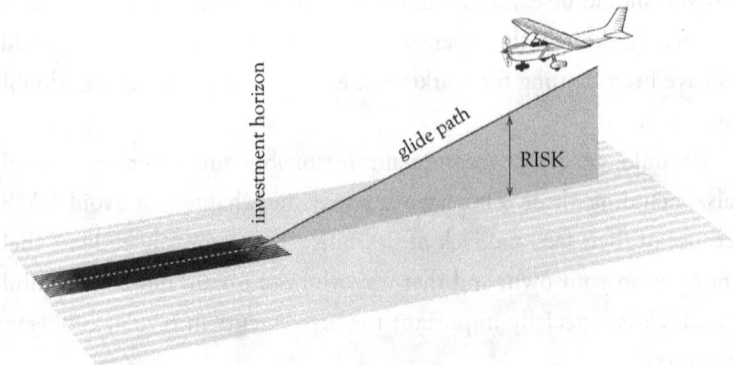

Figure 7.5 *Glide path of target-date fund*

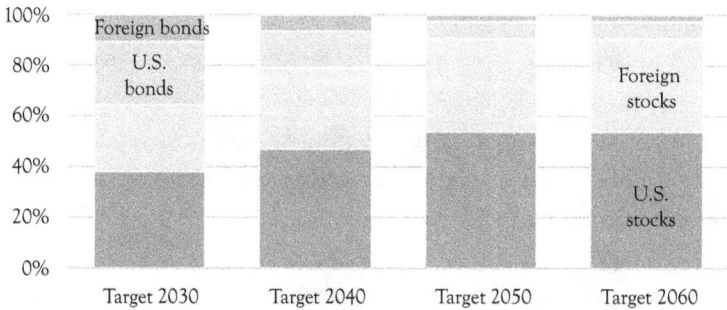

Figure 7.6 Four of Vanguard's target-date funds

end up with low-yield fixed income securities, which for longer invest-ment horizons are clearly inferior.

Note, though, that the designers of the target-date funds assume that the investors have most of their portfolios in the target-date funds. But that assumption is usually violated, in which case the target-date funds might not work quite as intended.

Figure 7.6 shows the composition of four of Vanguard's target-date funds (which Vanguard calls target retirement funds) as of February 2023. The fees for these are all reasonable, though you could still save some money by composing these on your own. I also believe the alloca-tions across asset types, including the glide path, are reasonable, though they could have included a small fraction of REITs as well. In short, I would be happy to endorse Vanguard's target-date funds as the default option for a retirement plan.

Target-Risk Funds

Target-risk funds, also known as lifestyle funds, differ from target-date funds in that their asset allocations remain constant over time. They seek to provide conservative, moderate, or aggressive risk allocations to suit investors' investment horizons and risk preferences. But, of course, as investors change their investment horizons, they should also change their risk allocations, so target-risk funds are not as "maintenance-free" as target-date funds. They are also not as popular as target-date funds.

Figure 7.7 shows the composition of Vanguard's four target-risk funds as of February 2023. Note that there are similarities between some of these target-risk funds and some of Vanguard's target-date funds. For example, the growth fund is almost identical to the target 2040 fund. Of course, the target fund will change over time and be more like the moderate growth fund after 10 years or so.

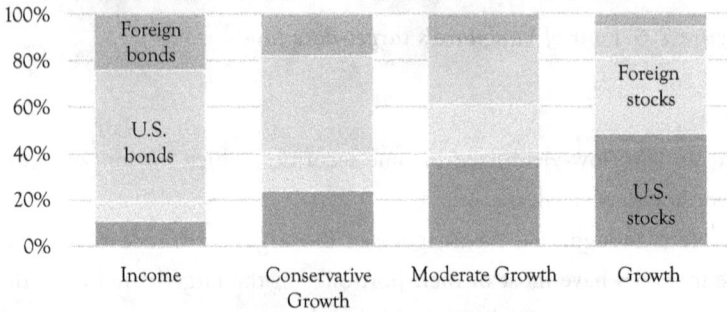

Figure 7.7 Vanguard's four target-risk funds

CHAPTER 8

Alternative Investments and Alternative Investment Accounts

Individuals are surrounded by both simple and exotic investment types and accounts. Earlier, we covered the basics of stocks and bonds and even funds. This chapter serves as an extension by covering more convoluted investment bundles, real estate, and specialized investment accounts.

The main objectives for this chapter are:

- Explore the features of more exotic investment types and accounts, as well as real estate.
- Learn which of the aforementioned are suitable for individuals and which are likely to be scams.

Permanent Life Insurance

The previous chapter discussed life insurance, with a focus on term life insurance. But a different type of life insurance product, *permanent life insurance*, includes a significant savings component, as Figure 8.1 shows. As a result, permanent life insurance comes with a much higher premium.

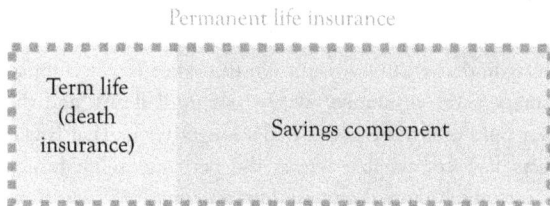

Figure 8.1 *The components of permanent life insurance*

Figure 8.2 shows the annual premiums for term life and permanent life insurance, assuming that the applicants are super preferred (meaning non-smokers with a superb medical record) and the death benefit is $500,000 (based on data from nerdwallet.com). Whereas a 20-year term life insurance will cost a very healthy 30-year-old individual a couple of hundred dollars a year, permanent life insurance costs 15 to 20 times more.[1]

As the name suggests, permanent life insurance does not expire, at least not as long as the policyholder continues to pay the premium. Furthermore, it accumulates cash value that generates a modest return, but the cash value might not accumulate in the first few years due to fees and commissions. There are three major categories of permanent life insurance:

- *Whole life* is the most common type of permanent life, and the two names are often used synonymously. Whole life provides a fixed but dismal return of 1 to 2 percent on the cash value.
- *Universal life* differs from whole life in that the policyholder has more flexibility to change the benefit level, the payment

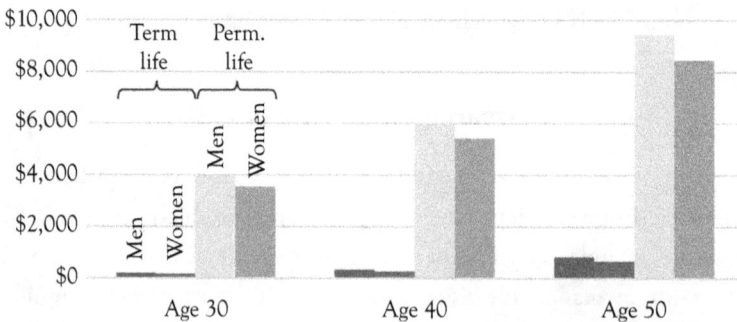

Figure 8.2 Annual premiums for super preferred applicants and death benefit of $500,000

---

[1] You might argue that a 20-year term life insurance is not comparable to the term for permanent life insurance, which lasts until death, and that the term life insurance would cost more had it had a longer term. That is true. But even if the products had comparable terms, the permanent life insurance would undoubtedly cost much more than term life insurance.

arrangement, and the premium. That also means that the accumulated cash value can be used to cover payments of premiums that the policyholder misses. An indexed universal life has a return on the cash value tied to (but not equal to) that of a stock index. The typical return is 3 to 4 percent.

- *Variable life* has more risky investment options and more variable return. The typical return is 4 to 5 percent.

A key feature with most contracts is that upon death, the cash value is taken by the insurance company. Thus, the policyholder should make sure the cash value is drained and redeployed later in life so it doesn't end up with the insurer.

How would you take out the cash value then?

- You can withdraw part of the cash value, but that reduces the death benefit. The reduction in death benefit is likely to equal the withdrawal for universal and variable life and exceed the withdrawal for whole life.
- You can surrender the whole policy to get the cash value. But that means that you give up the death benefit, and you might be charged a surrender fee.
- You can borrow against the cash value. But it sounds outrageous, right, to borrow against your own money and pay interest to do so? And, of course, the cash value is still where it was.
- Sell the policy to a third party that takes over future payments and becomes the new beneficiary. Those third parties seek to buy your contract at a deep discount if your remaining life expectancy is low so they can soon pocket the death benefit.

Overall, I fail to see the value in permanent life insurance products. Some would argue that high-income individuals benefit from their tax-deferred savings. But there are so many downsides: their fees and commissions are high; there is little need for death insurance beyond

Figure 8.3 Financial bait

the age of 60 (much less the entire life); the return on the cash value is poor; it is difficult to access the cash value; and the remaining cash value upon death goes to the insurer. Thus, I strongly recommend against these products—do not take the permanent life bait in Figure 8.3 from even the best insurance salesperson! You are better off keeping your insurance and investments separate by purchasing a term life policy and establishing a separate investment account that you control and no insurance company can take away from you.

Annuities

Annuities are another investment product that life insurance companies and other financial institutions offer. With a basic annuity, the investor (*annuitant*) pays a premium (or premiums) in exchange for a series of payments from the insurance company until death, as illustrated in Figure 8.4. In that sense, it is like Social Security benefits and defined benefit contribution retirement plans, in which the government and an employer, respectively, make payments from retirement until death.

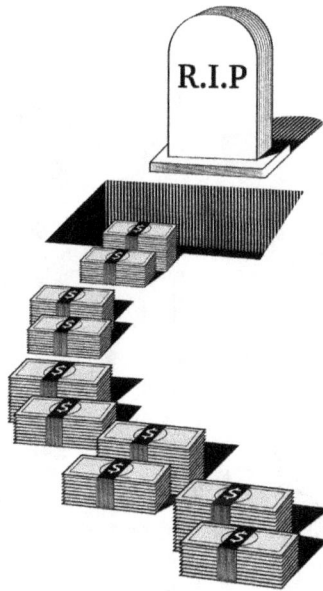

Figure 8.4 Annuity payments

However, annuities come in many variations, as Figure 8.5 shows. The investor could pay the insurance company in a lump sum or over time. Furthermore, the payments from the insurance company could (i) start immediately or be deferred, (ii) persist for a fixed period or the rest of the investor's life, and (iii) be fixed or tied to the performance of some investment or index.[2]

You might ask why life insurance companies sell annuities. It is not because they are similar to standard term life insurance contracts—the latter pay upon death, while typical annuities pay while you are alive. More likely, it is because typical annuities are the opposite of term life insurance contracts in the sense that premature death causes insurance companies to lose money on life insurance contracts and profit on annuities. Thus, annuities work as a hedge, or insurance if you will, for life insurance companies. Also, life insurance companies are skilled at estimating the time of death, which is useful when selling both life insurance and annuities.

---

[2] A couple could also purchase a *joint life annuity*, such that upon one spouse's death, the surviving spouse continues to receive benefits for life, either partially or in full.

Investor pays money to the insurance company

Could be one payment (*single-premium annuity*) or many payments across years

Accumulation phase

Could be no delay (*immediate*) or years of delay (*deferred*)

Payments could be fixed or tied to the performance of some investment or an index

Payout phase

Could be a fixed period (*annuity certain*) or until death (*straight life annuity*)

Investor receives money from the insurance company

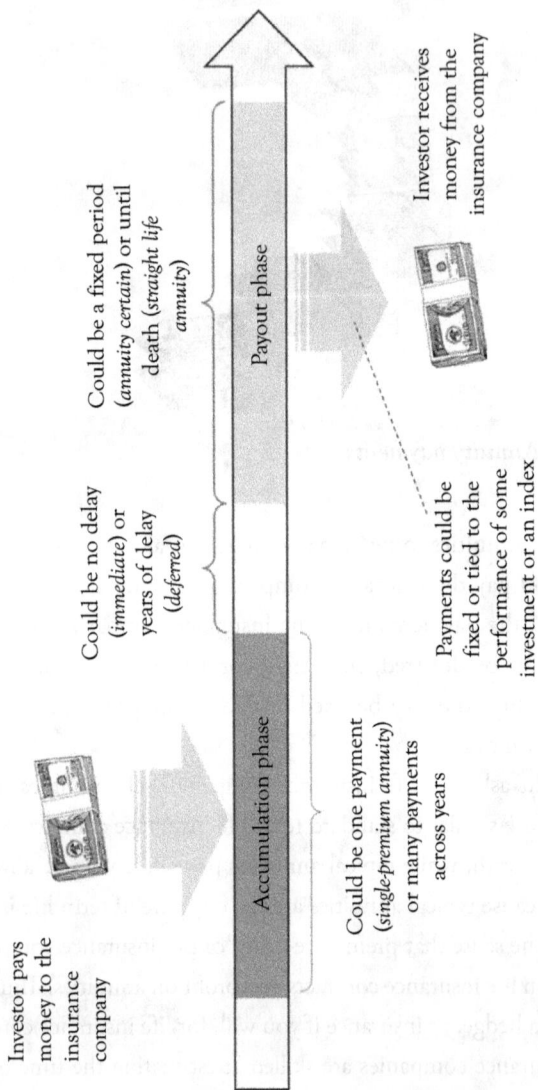

Figure 8.5 Common variations in annuities

Sales pitches stress that annuities come with tax benefits because the annuities are tax-deferred. But let's face it—the tax benefits are not that great:

- If the annuity is bought with pretax dollars inside a retirement account, for example, your 401(k) or IRA, the annuity payments are taxed at the employment income tax rate, just like other withdrawals from the retirement account. That means that annuities have no tax benefit over other investments inside the account.
- If the annuity is bought with after-tax dollars inside a Roth retirement account, there is no tax on the annuity payments. But, then again, there are no taxes on any withdrawals from the account, so annuities do not enjoy a tax advantage.
- If the annuity is bought with after-tax dollars outside your retirement account, the portion of the annuity payment that is deemed to be investment income (based on a so-called exclusion ratio) is taxed as ordinary income. This implies a couple of downsides:
  - A portion of the annuity payment is taxed at the investor's employment income tax rate, not the more favorable capital gains tax rate.
  - The investor has limited ability to defer taxation, which the following example shows.

Suppose that Anna just purchased an immediate annuity for $162,000 outside her retirement account that pays a life-time monthly income of $1,500. Given her age of 65, Anna has a life expectancy of 20 years based on the IRS actuarial table (search online for "Table V–Ordinary Life Annuities"). The expected return, defined as the total amount Anna is expected to receive, is $20 \times 12 \times \$1,500 = \$360,000$. The exclusion ratio is the investment in the contract divided by the expected return: $\$162,000/\$360,000 = 0.45$. That means that:

- $0.45 \times \$1,500 = \$675$ of her monthly payments are tax-free. (Note that $\$675 \times 12 \times 20$ equals the purchase price of $162,000.)

- $(1 - 0.45) \times \$1,500 = \$825$ of her monthly payments are
  taxable as ordinary income at the employment income tax rate.

In short, annuities have no incremental tax benefit inside tax-advantaged retirement accounts, while their tax benefits outside retirement accounts are, at best, modest, and you can likely do better tax-wise using the strategies outlined earlier for regular brokerage accounts.

Annuities also come with high fees, including commissions, ongoing expenses, and surrender charges on large withdrawals during the first 6 to 10 years. Furthermore, they often have convoluted terms that make them hard to value and compare to other investment products, but they are presented in ways that are deceptive to potential investors.

Consider a hypothetical (but realistic) equity-indexed annuity that is pitched as tracking the S&P 500 but guaranteed not to decrease in value. That sounds too good to be true, right? Indeed, it is—products that truly track the stock market cannot guarantee anything, so there must be a trade-off. The devil is, as always, in the details, as in Figure 8.6.

The more complete terms of the equity-indexed annuity show the following:

- The annuity tracks the S&P500. Note, however, that the S&P 500 index is a price index that does not include dividends.

Figure 8.6 *Annuity contract with devil in the details*

Thus, if you own all the stocks in the index or an ETF like SPY, the actual returns would be higher by about the dividend yield of some 2 percent.

- The minimum return is 0 percent, which option experts would refer to as a put option feature.
- The participation rate is 80 percent, meaning that you only get 80 percent of the S&P 500 return.
- The cap (i.e., maximum return) is 7 percent, which option experts would refer to as a short call option feature. Incidentally, this cap is on the high end of the norm of 3 to 7 percent.

To help understand these terms, I made a graph of the annual returns for the S&P 500 and the annuity if it had existed from 1994 to the present. This is depicted in Figure 8.7.

Based on this information, do you think you could assess the appeal of the annuity? Clearly, it has much less volatility than the S&P 500 index. However, it also has a much smaller average return; the average return for the annuity is 4.6 percent, compared to 9.5 percent for the S&P 500 and 11.5 percent for the S&P 500 with reinvested dividends.

When experts run simulations of actual annuities versus simpler investments, they find that annuities underperform in most cases. That is not surprising, given the fees embedded in annuities. Also, my general experience with financial products is that more convoluted terms disguise some weaknesses and are associated with worse performance.

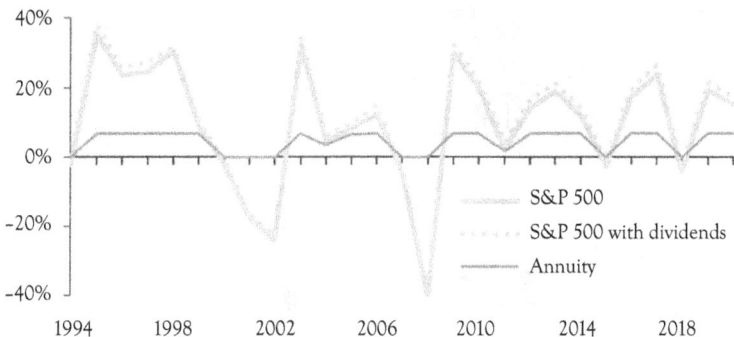

Figure 8.7 Annual returns for the S&P 500 and a hypothetical annuity

In conclusion, I recommend against buying annuities. Their returns net of fees are poor, while their tax benefits are overrated (and nonexistent inside a retirement account). If you are tantalized by their relative safety, you should rather invest a larger portion of your total investment in fixed-income securities.

Real Estate and Mortgage Financing

Real Estate as an Investment

Regardless of why you buy a house or condominium—for example, the pride of ownership, cost effectiveness, or the prospect for value appreciation—it is a significant investment. Figure 8.8 illustrates this investment. In most cases, the investment is funded with some savings and a large mortgage loan.

Due to the large mortgage, the real estate investment is heavily leveraged during the first several years, meaning that the equity in the house (i.e., the net investment, defined as the real estate value less the remaining mortgage) is small and volatile. In fact, if the housing market were to crash as it did in 2008 and you have put down little equity (say, less than 10 percent), the equity could very well evaporate entirely, and the mortgage could be

Figure 8.8 Investing in real estate

"underwater." If so, you could move out and cut your losses to your initial equity.[3]

Suppose that you bought a house for $250,000 financed with a mortgage of $200,000 (80 percent) and equity of $50,000 (20 percent). In this case, a 10 percent drop in the house value to $225,000 would cause your equity to drop by 50 percent to $25,000. Thus, with 20 percent equity financing, the house is leveraged five times, so any percentage change in the house value is magnified five times for the equity value.

However, as you pay down the mortgage, the real estate becomes a safer investment. Yet, unlike investments in stocks and bonds, it suffers from substantial information asymmetry and transaction costs that make it hard to sell on short notice at a fair price. Thus, you should view your real estate as a long-term investment that gets safer with time. Once you have paid off most of the mortgage, I regard real estate as safe as a fixed-income fund.[4]

Figure 8.9 shows the possible changes in the value of a house (starting at $250,000) and equity (starting at $50,000) over the 20-year period that the mortgage lasts. The mortgage declines steadily over time, while the equity

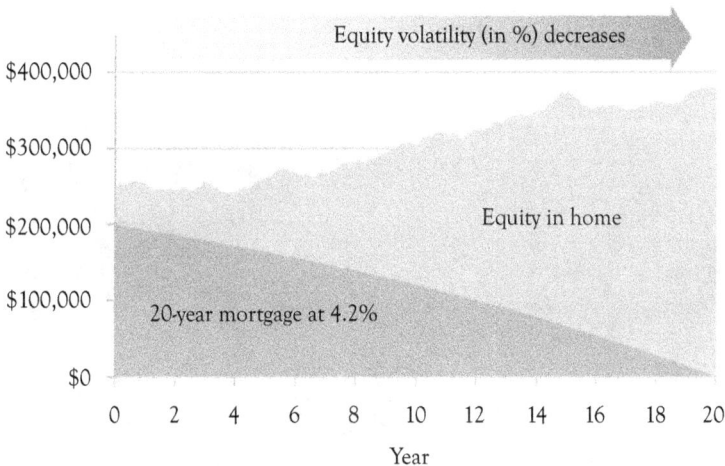

Figure 8.9 Possible changes in the total value and equity of a house

---

[3] However, such *strategic default* hurts your credit score and ability to get a future mortgage. You might instead stay in the house and keep making the mortgage payments, request a reduction in the loan principal, or request a loan modification to lengthen the maturity or reduce the interest rate.

[4] If you live in a volatile housing market like San Francisco, you probably disagree.

tends to increase in a jagged fashion. This would be a quite typical scenario for long-term homeowners who do not refinance their mortgage. The figure also illustrates that the equity volatility increases over time, though you might not see that at first glance. Think of it this way: while the house value volatility (in percent) is likely to be relatively steady, the volatility in the mortgage value is minimal, so when the mortgage is high, all the house value volatility becomes concentrated in the relatively small equity value.

Figure 8.10 shows the performance of the S&P 500 with dividends and the S&P CoreLogic Case–Shiller U.S. National Home Price Index from 1993 onward.[5] The figure also presents a five times leveraged home price index that represents homeowners' return on their equity investments if they had only 20 percent equity in their homes. The home price index has not performed nearly as well as the S&P 500, but it comes close when leveraged five times. It is harder to compare the volatilities, because the S&P 500 shows large month-to-month fluctuations while the home index has more prolonged fluctuations. Nevertheless, the figure reiterates that investments in real estate are quite risky when financed with a large mortgage loan, and they become fairly safe (with a correspondingly low return) when the loan is repaid.

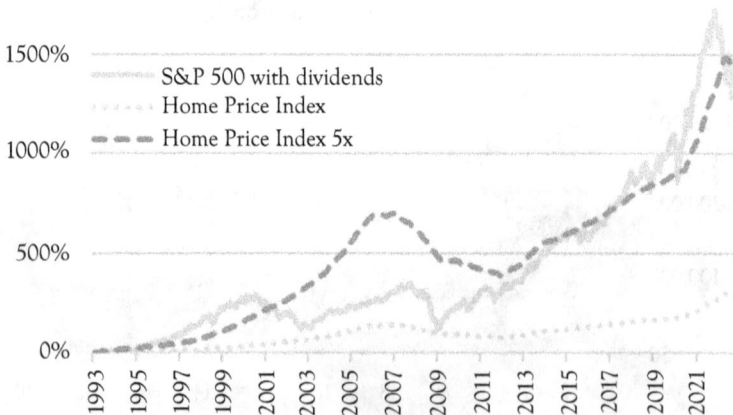

Figure 8.10 The performance of the S&P 500 and the home price index

---

[5] This home price index is a composite of single-family home price indices for the nine U.S. Census divisions. It is updated monthly based on three-month moving averages, so it likely exhibits less monthly volatility than the true home price volatility. Furthermore, it does not capture the benefits (being able to live in the house or rent it out) and costs (maintenance, insurance, taxes, and mortgage interests) of having the house.

Lastly, some words about taxation when owning real estate. One substantial benefit of owning versus renting is that interest on up to $750,000 in mortgage debt is deductible from taxes. This is essentially a government subsidy for home ownership. On the flip side, when you own real estate, you must pay annual property taxes that could be as high as 2 percent of the value.

Tax on Gain

When you sell real estate, you must in principle pay taxes on any realized capital gains. If you have lived in the house/condo for two of the last five years, you get a capital gains exemption of either $250,000 (for single filers) or $500,000 (married filing jointly).[6] However, you can only get this exemption once every two years. You may also qualify for a partial exemption if you sold the home because of work, health, or an "unforeseeable event."

When estimating the gain, you can deduct the costs of home improvements (i.e., the home improvement costs are added to the cost basis of the property). You can even deduct costs of smaller improvements, like installing new windows or a central heating system, but not costs of ongoing maintenance and repairs. Thus, you should retain and organize receipts from all home improvement projects.

Furthermore, as with realized capital gains on stocks, you can strategically offset capital losses on stocks. Thus, in years when the market is down, you should consider selling stocks with large capital losses and carry those losses forward to the year when you anticipate selling a property at a large gain. But, as noted earlier, beware of the wash-sale rule when reinvesting the proceeds from the stock sales.

Mortgage Financing

Mortgages, illustrated in Figure 8.11, have either a fixed or adjustable interest rate. Fixed-rate mortgages (FRMs) have a set interest rate for the duration of the loan. Adjustable-rate mortgages (ARMs) usually have a

---

[6] If the capital gain is expected to exceed $25,000, it might make sense for several household members to co-own the property. This could be arranged via gifts, in which case the cost basis is transferred to the recipient.

Figure 8.11 Mortgage financing

fixed rate for a period up to 10 years, after which it varies with market rates, for example, Treasury yields.

Which is better? Arguably, both the cost and risk matter for borrowers:

- Cost: On the one hand, the ARM rate is set below the FRM rate, at least initially, and ARMs are, therefore, generally less costly. On the other hand, the FRM comes with a valuable refinancing option if market rates fall, which we explore later.
- Risk: Because FRMs protect borrowers from unexpected increases in market rates, many would argue that ARMs are riskier. However, the increasing market rates generally go hand in hand with increasing inflation, which lightens the burden of loan repayment. That is, the increase in salaries that tend to come with inflation (albeit with a lag) covers any increase in interest payments.

In sum, the choice is not clear-cut. Many economists contend that ARMs are better unless interest rates are very low, but I am reluctant to give categorical advice. In any event, most loans in the United States, perhaps 85 percent, have a fixed interest, and the rest of this section focuses on those.

As a borrower, you must pay more than the regular interest rate, including (i) an *origination fee* for evaluating and preparing the mortgage loan and perhaps, (ii) *discount points* to reduce the loan's interest rate, where the cost of one discount point equals 1 percent of the loan amount, and

(iii) *mortgage insurance* if the down payment is less than 20 percent. Based on the interest rate and other loan costs, we can calculate the annual percentage rate (APR), which you can view as an all-in-cost of the mortgage.[7]

When you first get a mortgage, you must choose the term length. Typical terms are 15, 20, and 30 years. Longer terms obviously mean smaller monthly payments, but you accumulate equity more slowly. Also, long-term loans tend to come with higher interest rates. So, what term should you choose? You should first make sure that you can cover regular expenses and max out your contributions to tax-advantaged retirement accounts. If you still believe that you can comfortably make the more aggressive payments associated with shorter-term loans, you can consider a shorter term. Incidentally, if you choose a longer term, you may still pay off the loan earlier.

There are, however, also other events and decisions to be made during the term of the loan related to prepayments and refinancing. But first, we should cover some basic mortgage math. I hope you bear with me if you think you will run into these situations.

Perpetuities and Annuities

A *perpetuity* is a cash flow that lasts forever. The present value (*PV*) of one cash flow (*CF*) that we get next year, given an interest rate (*r*), can be written as $CF/(1 + r)$, and the present value of that cash flow lasting forever is CF/r.

An *annuity*, on the other hand, is a cash flow that runs for several periods but not forever.[8] Thus, an annuity that runs from year 1 through year *t* is the same as a perpetuity starting in year 1, less a perpetuity starting in year *t*+1, as illustrated in Figure 8.12.

---

[7] The convention for mortgage loans is to provide the interest rate as the monthly interest rate multiplied by 12. Standard finance books refer to this as an APR (annual percentage rate). However, in the mortgage world, APR refers to the annual rate that also includes other loan costs. Note that this does not capture compounding within a year, so the effective all-in-cost per year is even higher.

[8] This is the technical definition of an annuity. But earlier we also used the term annuity to refer to some financial products that make payments for a certain period, so I understand if you get confused.

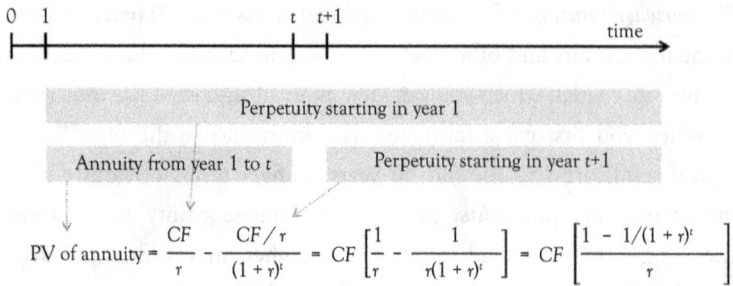

Figure 8.12 Valuation of an annuity

$$PV \text{ of annuity} = \frac{CF}{r} - \frac{CF/r}{(1+r)^t} = CF\left[\frac{1}{r} - \frac{1}{r(1+r)^t}\right] = CF\left[\frac{1 - 1/(1+r)^t}{r}\right]$$

In Excel, you can simply use the function =PV($\cdot$) to get the PV of an annuity. Also, if you instead need to solve for the regular cash flow payments, CF, or the interest rate, r, in the annuity formula, you can use the Excel functions =PMT($\cdot$) and =RATE($\cdot$), respectively. I will demonstrate the use of these Excel functions in an example later.

Amortization

Amortization shows how a loan is paid off over time. Let me illustrate with a simple example. Suppose that you borrow $10,000 at 12 percent to be repaid in four equal annual installments. Using the annuity formula, we can set the present value to $10,000, r to 12 percent, and t to 4, and then solve for CF, which equals $3.292. In Excel, it would simply be: =PMT(0.12,4,-10000).

Next, let us calculate how much is interest and principal in each year. To do that, I have made the amortization table in Figure 8.13 along with boxes that provide the calculations for the first couple of years.

	0	1	2	3	4
Balance	$10,000	$7,908	$5,564	$2,940	$0
Interest		$1,200	$949	$668	$353
Principal		$2,092	$2,343	$2,625	$2,940
Total		$3,292	$2,292	$3,292	$3,292

$10,000 × 12% $10,000 − $2,092 $7,908 × 12% $7,908 − $2,343

$3,292 − $1,200 $3,292 − $949

Figure 8.13 Amortization

Note that the interest row could alternatively be solved in Excel as: =IPMT(0.12,per,4,-10000), where per refers to the year, that is, either 1, 2, 3, or 4. Also note that the remaining balance at the end of year 4 is $0, which means that our calculations are very likely to be correct.

Example of Estimating Monthly Payments and APR for a Fixed-Rate Mortgage

Consider a $200,000, 20-year FRM with a 4.2 percent interest rate. That means that there are 20 × 12 = 240 monthly payments, and the monthly interest rate is 4.2%/12 = 0.35%.

We can solve for the monthly payments using the aforementioned annuity formula or the PMT(·) function in Excel: =PMT(0.042/12,20*12,200000) = **–$1,233**. If we know the monthly payments, we can alternatively solve for the monthly interest rate, r, using the annuity formula or the RATE(·) function in Excel and then multiply by 12 months to get the quoted annual rate: =RATE(20*12,-1233,200000)*12 = **4.2%**.

Now, let us also consider the fees to get a more complete picture. The loan has two discount points (meaning 2 percent of loan) and a 1 percent origination fee, for total fees of: 2% × $200,000 + 1% × $200,000 = $6,000.[9] That means that the borrower only gets $200,000 – $6,000 = $194,000. If we include the fees in our calculation, we get: =RATE(20*12,-1233,194000)*12 = **4.56%**.[10] This is what the mortgage world refers to as the APR.[11] Thus, the fees raise the annualized borrowing cost by 4.56% – 4.2% = 0.36%.[12] This is illustrated in Figure 8.14.

We could readily use this procedure to compare to an alternative FRM with the same initial loan amount of $200,000 and a 20-year term but a

---

[9] Discount points are optional fees that you pay to reduce the interest rate (sometimes referred to as "buying down the rate"). If you buy one discount point, you will pay a fee of 1 percent of the mortgage loan, and the lender will typically cut the rate by 0.25 percent, though the magnitude of the cut varies.

[10] Incidentally, the APR would be the same here if we borrowed the loan costs, but in that case, the payments would be higher at $1,271.

[11] The effective all-in-cost per year that also considers compounding is $(1 + 4.56\%/12)^{12} - 1 = 4.66\%$.

[12] This is larger than the fees of 3 percent divided by 20 years due to the time value of money effect.

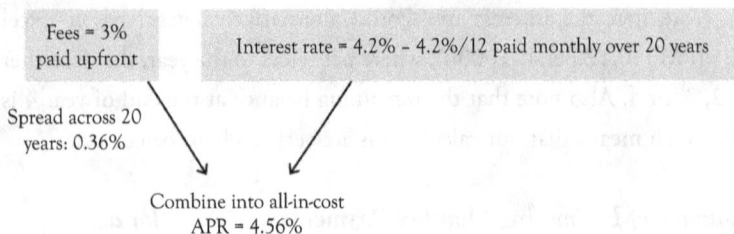

Fees = 3% paid upfront

Interest rate = 4.2% – 4.2%/12 paid monthly over 20 years

Spread across 20 years: 0.36%

Combine into all-in-cost
APR = 4.56%

Figure 8.14 All-in-cost of mortgage

4.4 percent interest rate, 1 percent origination fee, and no points. First, we solve for the monthly payments: =PMT(0.044/12,20*12,200000) = **–$1,255**. Then, we solve for APR: =RATE(20*12,-1255,198000)*12 = **4.52%**. That means that this loan has better overall terms, as indicated by the APR of 4.52 percent versus 4.56 percent, despite the greater monthly payments.

The examples illustrate that we cannot directly compare the quoted interest rates—that would be like comparing apples to oranges. For the apples-to-apples comparison in Figure 8.15, we must calculate the all-in-costs that consider both interest rates and various fees.

Example of Prepayment and Refinancing

Let us return to the $200,000, 20-year FRM with a 4.2 percent interest rate, 1 percent origination fee, and two discount points. A portion of the amortization table is given in Figure 8.16.

Suppose that after five years, or 5 × 12 = 60 months, we are considering prepaying the loan. There might be various reasons for the prepayment,

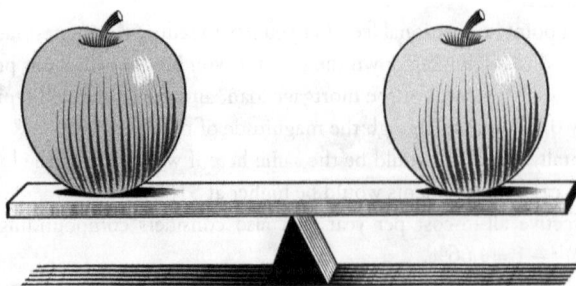

Figure 8.15 Apple-to-apple comparison

	0	1	2	• • •	60	• • •	239	240
Balance	$200,000	$199,467	$198,932		$164,474		$1,229	$0
Interest		$700	$698		$578		$9	$4
Principal		$533	$535		$655		$1,225	$1,229
Total		$1,233	$1,233		$1,233		$1,233	$1,233

(Above the "60" column:) Could simply estimate as = PV (0.042/12,12*15,-1233)

Figure 8.16 Partial amortization table

including the sale of the house or as part of a refinancing of the loan. You can see from the amortization table that the remaining balance after five years is **$164,474**, which you could also have calculated in Excel as =PV(0.042/12,12*15,-1233).

As illustrated in Figure 8.17, the APR for those first five years is =RATE(5*12,-1233,194000,-164474)*12 = **4.94%**. In comparison, the APR for the remaining 15 years is =RATE(15*12,-1233,164474)*12 = 4.20% because there are no further fees during that period. The reason why the APR of 4.94 percent for the first five years is higher than the APR for the entire 20-year period of 4.52 percent is that we get the effect of the fees concentrated in a shorter period.

Suppose further that after five years, the mortgage rate for 15-year mortgages dropped from 4.0 percent (slightly lower than the 20-year rate of 4.2 percent) to 3.5 percent. Should we refinance assuming a refinancing cost of 3 percent?

The remaining balance after five years is $164,474. Let us also assume that we borrow the fees of 3 percent, so there is no cash outlay at the time of refinancing. That means the new loan would be in the amount of $164,474/(1 − 0.03) = $169,560. We can then estimate the new payments as =PMT(0.035/12,12*15,169560) = **−$1,212**, meaning that we save $1,233 − $1,212 = $21 per month. What is the total value of the monthly savings? The total savings across 12 × 15 = 180 months is $21 ×

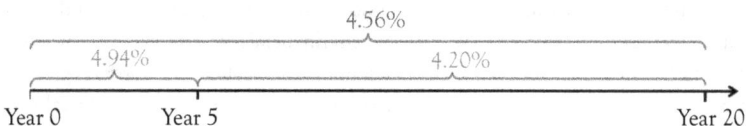

Figure 8.17 APR for various periods

180 = \$3,780, and, more importantly, the present value of these savings is =PV(0.035/12,12*15,-21) = \$2,937. Based on the monthly savings, you could argue that we should refinance.[13]

Generally, it does not make sense to refinance frequently due to the fees; in most cases, we really only have one shot at refinancing. Thus, if we refinance now, we essentially use up our option to refinance (unless the rate were to fall a lot more). The implication is that we should not refinance as soon as we can lower the payments; we might want to wait until we can get substantially lower payments.[14]

Suppose that in the next year, the 15-year rate (and, roughly, the 14-year rate if you could find one) will either remain constant, increase to 4 percent, or fall to 3 percent, as shown in Figure 8.18. If we refinance next year at the same rate of 3.5 percent, our monthly savings would be \$17, so we would be better off refinancing today. But if we refinance next year at the rate of 3 percent, our monthly savings would be \$56, for a total present value of \$7,674, which is obviously better.[15]

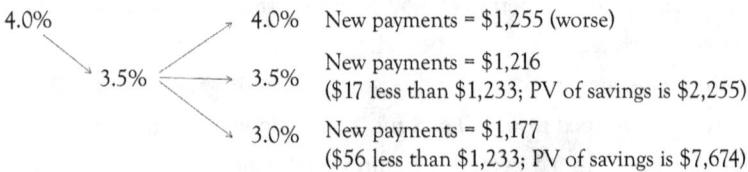

```
4.0%                    4.0%   New payments = $1,255 (worse)

                               New payments = $1,216
         3.5%           3.5%   ($17 less than $1,233; PV of savings is $2,255)

                        3.0%   New payments = $1,177
                               ($56 less than $1,233; PV of savings is $7,674)
```

Figure 8.18 Possible interest rate scenarios

---

[13] This assumes that we will remain in the house for the next 15 years. If we move out just one year after the refinancing event, we will lose money on the refinancing despite the savings of \$21 × 12 = \$252 on the payments for one year. The loss is a result of the balance of the new loan of \$160,810 (=PV(3.5%/12,14*12, -1212.16)) at the time of the move, which is \$4,380 higher than what the balance of the old loan of \$156,430 (=PV(4.2%/12,14*12,-1233.14)) would have been at the same time.

[14] You might be able to reduce the interest rate with a so-called rate modification on your current loan for about a thousand dollars instead of undertaking a more comprehensive and expensive refinancing. To do so, inform your mortgage lender that you are considering refinancing with a different financial institution and ask whether they offer a rate modification process to retain the loan, albeit at a lower rate.

[15] Some of you might recognize that we should also discount the present value of the savings next year one year back to properly compare to the present value of the savings we could get this year. That is true. And if we do that, the present value of the savings as of today is \$7,674/1.035 = \$7,414.

We could make this more complex by thinking about what could happen in two years, and we could even extend this to a multiyear simulation. But let us stop here and digest what we already have. If the probabilities next year of the three interest rate scenarios are similar, I would take a chance on a bigger payday next year. In general, whether you should refinance today comes down to (i) the monthly savings, (ii) how many monthly payments remain, (iii) what might happen to future rates, and (iv) whether you are likely to move before the end of the mortgage. As a rule of thumb, I would say that you should not refinance unless the present value of the savings is at least a couple of thousand dollars and you are unlikely to move. In any event, now you have the tools to make a more informed decision.

Concept Test—The Cost of Moving

It is costly to move, especially if we must sell a house and buy another one, as in Figure 8.19. The typical fee to real estate agents alone is 6 percent of the transaction price. What if the interest rates also increased since we got the mortgage on the house we are selling?

Suppose that both the new house and the old house are valued at roughly $250,000. Further, suppose that our old house had a $200,000, 20-year FRM with a 4.2 percent interest rate and 15 years left until maturity. From our calculation in an earlier subsection, we know that the monthly payments are $1,233 then. The interest rates have since risen, so we currently must pay 5.5 percent for a 15-year mortgage with total fees (origination fees and discount points) of 3 percent. How much will it cost us to refinance?

Figure 8.19 Moving from one house to another

We would first have to prepay the old mortgage at $164,474, which, as earlier, we can get from Excel as =PV(0.042/12,12*15,-1233). If we also borrow the fees of 3 percent, the new loan would be in the amount of $164,474/(1 − 0.03) = $169,560, and the new payments would be =PMT(0.055/12,12*15,169560) = −$1,385, for an increase of $1,385 − $1,233 = $152. The present value of paying an incremental $152 for each of the next 12 × 15 = 180 months is =PV(0.035/12,12*15,-152) = **$18,602**. That represents $18,602/$250,000 = 7.4% of the value of the house. So perhaps it would make more sense to stay in the old house with the better mortgage terms?

Reverse Mortgages

Over the years, homeowners accumulate equity in their homes as they pay down the mortgage, and for many, this equity represent their largest savings. A *reverse mortgage* allows homeowners of at least 62 years old to tap into the equity that they have accumulated in their homes, as Figure 8.20 illustrates. It is usually described as a way to borrow against your home equity. But I consider it more of a sale of your home, where you receive payments upfront and get to live in the house for the rest of your life or until you decide to move.

Figure 8.20 Reverse mortgage

Here is roughly how it works. Suppose that a senior needs cash but most of her savings are tied up as equity in her house, and she wishes to continue to stay in the house. Assuming that she has paid down most of her original mortgage, she can use a reverse mortgage to receive either (i) an immediate lump sum, (ii) fixed monthly payments for a certain period, for example, until she dies, or (iii) a line of credit. However, she only receives about a half to two-thirds of her equity in the house, depending on, for example, her age. The loan, along with a hefty interest, will be repaid when she moves or dies. The money for the repayment usually comes from selling the house, and any remaining equity goes to the estate.

Homeowners are still required to pay property taxes and homeowners insurance, use the property as their principal residence, and maintain the property. Otherwise, they could default, and the lender could foreclose on the property. This is a substantial risk in practice. While many lenders have been fined for saying that foreclosure cannot occur with reverse mortgages, the historical data show that close to 20 percent of reverse mortgages go into default (vs 2 to 3 percent of standard mortgages).

Not only do seniors who use reverse mortgages run a substantial risk of eviction, but the financial terms (including the upfront costs and interest rates) of reverse mortgages are confusing and much worse than they are for standard mortgages. Thus, reverse mortgages should be avoided. Unfortunately, there might be many seniors who are "house rich, cash poor" and wish to stay in their house for the rest of their lives. In those cases, reverse mortgages might be a necessary evil, but the homeowners should at least make sure to regularly pay property taxes and insurance premiums to avoid default.

College Savings Accounts

College has become increasingly expensive and can put a large dent in the savings of students' families. This requires substantial college savings, as Figure 8.21 illustrates. There is, however, a silver lining: 529 savings plans, also called college savings accounts.

Figure 8.21 College savings

A 529 plan works much like a Roth 401(k), in that you (i) contribute after-tax money to the account, (ii) select investments from a menu of mutual funds and ETFs, and (iii) withdraw the money tax-free. The only condition for the tax-free withdrawal is that the money covers qualified education expenses, including college expense and K-12 tuition.[16] In addition, more than 30 states allow you to take a state tax deduction for your contribution.

Most states offer a 529 plan, but you are not constrained to using the plan of your home state or using only one plan. Because each plan offers a different menu of investments, you should examine several plans before making selection(s). However, a few state plans have state residency requirements and do not permit individuals from other states to open an account, and most states that allow state tax deductions require the contributions to be made to the home state plan to be eligible for those deductions.

There is no annual contribution limit, but each state has an aggregate contribution limit of roughly $250,000 to $500,000. Furthermore, states that allow state tax deductions have annual limits on those deductions.

---

[16] Most other withdrawals are subject to taxes (on investment income) and a 10 percent penalty.

When you open an account for, say, your child or your grandchild, you assign that individual to be the beneficiary. Thus, with several children, you should open several accounts. Importantly, you have the flexibility to change the beneficiary later to another qualifying family member, like the beneficiary's sibling or child.

The SECURE Act of 2022 offers an alternative way to tap into any unused funds that are "stuck" in a 529 plan. Starting in 2024, the funds can be rolled over to a Roth IRA for the beneficiary. However, there are some limitations. First, the plan must have been open for at least 15 years. Second, rollovers are subject to annual Roth contribution limits (but they are not subject to Roth IRA income limits). Third, the lifetime rollover is limited to $35,000. Fourth, the rollover must come from earnings and contributions that are at least five years old.

In sum, college savings accounts are excellent savings vehicles for anybody who expects to assist a family member or friend with college expenses in the near or distant future. In fact, the further into the future, the better, because the longer the money grows tax-free.

Health Savings Accounts

HSAs and Their Supercharged Tax Benefits

Health Savings Accounts (HSAs) are saving accounts to be used for qualified health care expenses, including medical, dental, and mental health services. They come with significant tax advantages, including tax-deductible contributions, tax-free growth, *and* tax-free withdrawals. But to be eligible, you must be enrolled in a High-Deductible Health Plan (HDHP), which have lower premiums and higher deductibles (at least $1,500 for individuals and $3,000 for families in 2023).[17] Thus, ironically, HSAs and their accompanying HDHPs might be most suitable for relatively healthy people.

---

[17] You can think of HSAs as self-insurance for health expenses, and because health insurance with high deductibles covers only a portion of the health expenses, some extra self-insurance is sensible.

For 2023, the contribution limit is $3,850 for individuals ($4,850 for those over 55) and $7,750 for families.[18] Contributions are effectively made pretax. For example, an employer can make pretax deductions from the payroll, and this is excluded from the employee's taxable income. Or you can contribute after-tax money and then deduct it from your taxable income.

In addition, withdrawals are tax-free if they are used for *qualified* health care expenses. That makes HSAs better than other tax-advantaged accounts we have examined, which are either accepting before-tax contributions (like IRAs) *or* tax-free withdrawals (like Roth IRAs), but not both.

If you withdraw funds for *nonqualified* expenses, you pay taxes based on your employment income tax, and if you are less than 65 years old, you also must pay a 20 percent penalty. That means that if you do not have any health care expenses and wait until you reach the age of 65, you can essentially use the HSA as a "sleeper" or "stealth" IRA account with the added benefit of not having any required minimum distribution (RMD). In that sense, I consider an HSA to be no worse than an IRA account in the worst case (not including cases where you must make withdrawals before age 65).

Finally, how do HSAs compare to FSAs (Flexible Savings Accounts), which many employers offer, including the University of Iowa? First, you cannot have both because FSAs require a Preferred Provider Organization (PPO) health plan, so you might have to make a choice. The most important difference between them is that FSAs are "use it or lose it" accounts, meaning that you must spend the money contributed to the account on health care expenses during the same year.[19] In contrast, HSAs are portable and can accumulate funds over

---

[18] Young adult children (under age 26) who are still covered by their parents' HDHP but are not claimed as dependents on their parents' tax returns can contribute to their separate HSA.

[19] Depending on your plan, you might be able roll a measly $550 of the over to the next year. But if you are stuck with substantial funds in your FSA account at the end of the year, there are at least plenty of ideas on the Internet for how to spend it in a hurry, ranging from eye exams/glasses to massage guns and sunscreen lotion.

an extended period. That is beneficial because you might not have health care expenses every year, and you can strategically allow funds to grow tax-free. Thus, if you are healthy enough to tolerate an HDHP, I recommend an HSA.

Concept Test—Reimbursement Postponement

Manny, who fancies himself the "money guy" in the household, has thought of a new scheme to extract more value from the family's HSA. He has just paid $1,000 of medical expenses. Instead of immediately getting reimbursement from the HSA account, he has decided to wait so that the money can grow tax-free in the meantime, given that the HSA has no reimbursement deadline. Figure 8.22 illustrates this postponement. His wife, Mona, has doubts. First, she believes that Manny is likely to lose the receipt for the expense. Second, she claims that the HSA account is likely to grow so much that it will likely exceed their qualified health care expenses, meaning that at some point they will have to pay ordinary income taxes on withdrawals from the account. Third, she argues that the money can be invested in a reasonably tax-efficient way outside the HSA account. Who is right?

The answer depends on the assumptions. Let us start with a simple setting in which the money can be invested in an ETF with trivial dividends

Figure 8.22 Postponing the reimbursement

either inside or outside the HSA. Furthermore, the ETF quintuples in value over the next decades until Manny and Mona need the funds. Also assume that the capital gains tax rate is 15 percent and the employment income tax rate is 25 percent.

Scenario 1—Manny gets immediate reimbursement: The $1,000 is invested in a regular brokerage account and grows to a value of $5,000. When withdrawn, the capital gains tax is 15 percent × $4,000 = $600, so the value after taxes is $5,000 − $600 = $4,400.

Scenario 2—Manny postpones the reimbursement: The money grows to $5,000 inside the HSA. When Manny later gets the $1,000 reimbursement, the $1,000 is withdrawn tax-free. But if he also wants to withdraw the remaining $4,000, he will have to pay ordinary income taxes of 25% × $4,000 = $1,000. Thus, the net value is $5,000 − $1,000 = $4,000.

So far, Mona seems to be correct. However, the assumptions can easily be tweaked in either direction. For example, if the family has more qualified health care expenses in the future than is in the HSA account, the entire $5,000 in scenario 2 can be withdrawn tax-free, and Manny would be correct. On the other hand, the capital gains tax in scenario 1 can be reduced by realizing capital losses along with capital gains. In short, there is no clear answer.

Wrapping Up With Financial Scams

Many financial products originate with great ideas for how to improve individuals' financial health and security. For example, an annuity that lasts the rest of your life is a great idea for people who need certainty and assurance. Similarly, a reverse mortgage that transforms home equity to funds to be spent during retirement is a great idea for individuals who lack other savings and would prefer not to move.

Unfortunately, instead of offering products that deliver on these ideas, the financial industry routinely exploits individuals' naivete and anxiety about their finances by selling convoluted and expensive financial products that have the appearance of helping people. These products simply fail to deliver what they at first seem to promise, or they are ridiculously expensive, or both.

I believe that the scams in the financial world include most permanent life insurance contracts, annuities, and reverse mortgages. They should be in the same category of rarely to be used products as extended warranties, payday loans, and snake oil. Figure 8.23 drives home this point.

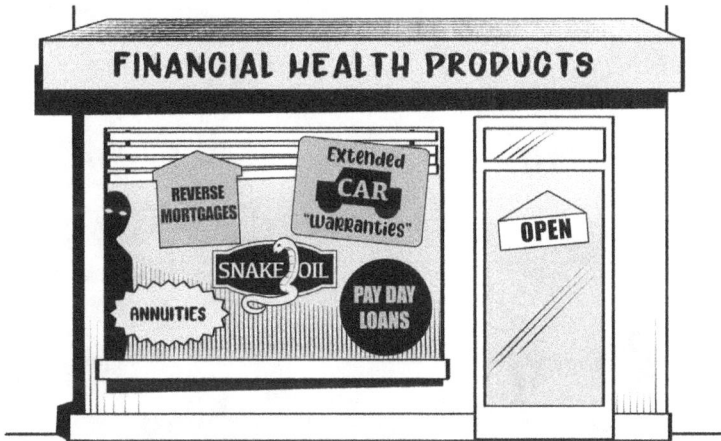

Figure 8.23 Financial health products store

CHAPTER 9

Asset Allocation and Retirement Planning

Most individuals accumulate wealth during their working years and deplete wealth during their retirement years, as Figure 9.1 depicts. The rates of accumulation and depletion depend on many factors, including:

- The income level during working years;
- The expenses, both during working years and during retirement;
- The retirement age; and
- How the savings are invested, also known as *asset allocation*.

A main goal is obviously to have savings that provide for a comfortable retirement free of financial worries. Another goal might be to leave wealth to heirs and charitable organizations.

To ensure that these goals are within reach requires a careful and tailor-made analysis that considers all the factors mentioned earlier, including variations in the investment returns. Naturally, it is impossible

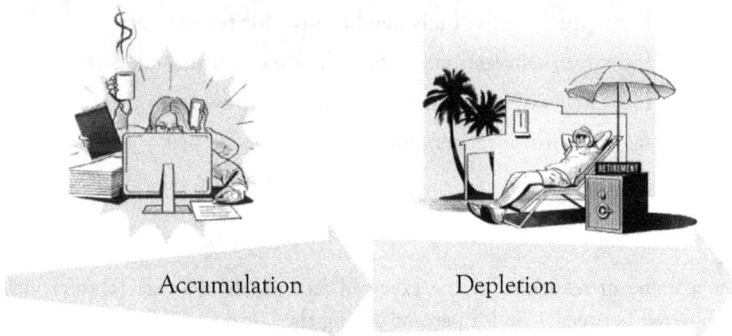

Figure 9.1 Accumulation and depletion of funds

to show this for all possible situations. In this section, I will instead show a more generic analysis that provides general insight into the implications of various savings, retirement, and investment decisions for income available during retirement.

In my analysis, I assume that we make annual investments in either a low-risk portfolio (with an expected annual return of 5 percent and a standard deviation of 7 percent) or a high-risk portfolio (with an expected return of 8 percent and a standard deviation of 14 percent) until retirement, and that we make annual withdrawal during retirement.[1] With higher inflation, one could expect higher interest rates and higher returns than I have used, but then one should also consider greater deterioration in purchasing power of a dollar over time. The appendix shows how you can run these types of simulations on your own (using your own assumptions), and there are also online tools that can do it for you.

I have ignored taxes in my analysis for simplicity. You can therefore think of the annual investments as after-tax money that is invested in a Roth account. Of course, you know by now that if the investments were made in a non-Roth retirement account instead, you would have to pay taxes on the withdrawals based on your income tax rate, and if the investments were made in a regular brokerage account, you would have to pay taxes on periodic dividend/interest income and on realized capital gains.

The main objectives for this chapter are:

- Explore the effects of savings behavior and asset allocation on investments available for retirement.
- Develop a sense for:
  - How much individuals need to save for retirement;
  - How much investment risk individuals should take; and
  - How aggressively individuals can withdraw from their savings during retirement.

---

[1] As a frame of reference for the expected returns, the 10-year Treasury yield has hovered between 1 and 4 percent during the last decade. Furthermore, the expected return for the S&P 500 index should roughly equal the Treasury yield plus a risk-premium of 6 to 7 percent, so about 8 to 10 percent.

Accumulation of Wealth

Annual Investments of $10,000

In this subsection, I examine the accumulation of wealth in the two alternative portfolios assuming annual investments of $10,000.[2] With annual investments, the investments that are made in early years are long-term, and the investments that are made shortly before retirement are short-term. In that sense, we have a combination of short-term and long-term investments, but more of the investments become long-term with more time until retirement.

I first simulated possible outcomes after 20 years, at which point the total investments in either the low-risk or high-risk portfolios equal $10,000 × 20 = $200,000. Figure 9.2 shows the distributions for the values of the two portfolios. The low-risk portfolio value has a 99 percent confidence interval between $215,000 and $543,000, and the average is $347,000. In comparison, the high-risk portfolio value has a 99 percent confidence interval between $178,000 and $1,188,000, and the average is $494,000.

Most people save for close to 40 years, and many even might get close to 50 years. After 40 years, the total investments equal $10,000 × 40 = 400,000. As shown in Figure 9.3, the low-risk portfolio value at that point

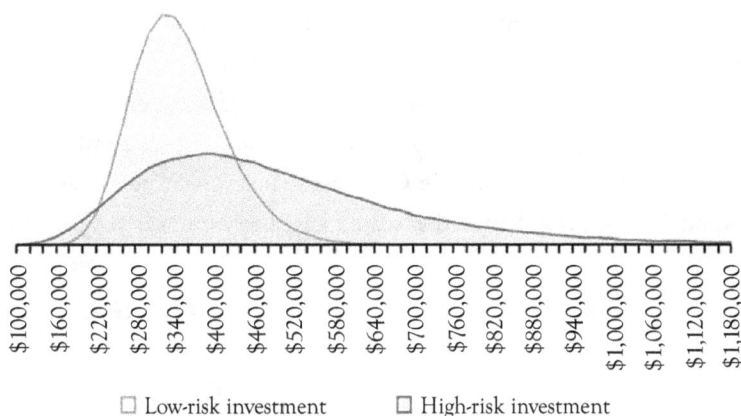

☐ Low-risk investment   ☐ High-risk investment

Figure 9.2 Values after 20 years

---

[2] If you want to know what the implication of, say, saving $20,000 annually instead, you can simply multiply all the results by a factor of 2.

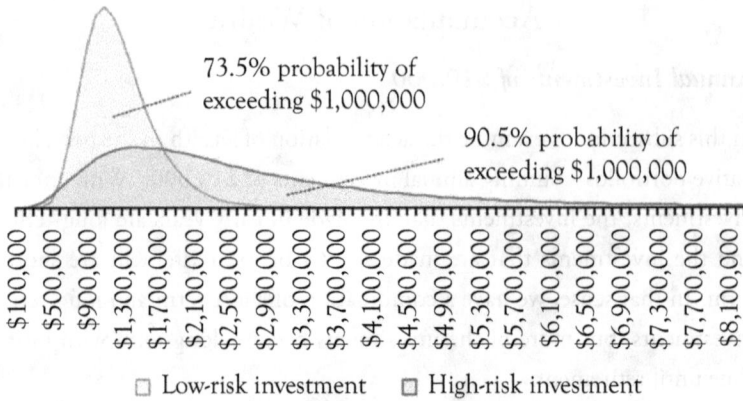

Figure 9.3 Values after 40 years

has a 99 percent confidence interval between $609,000 and $2,478,000, and the average is $1,268,000, while the high-risk portfolio value has a 99 percent confidence interval between $547,000 and $10,288,000, and the average is $2,799,000. Also, the probabilities that the values of the low-risk and high-risk portfolios exceed $1,000,000 are 73.5 and 90.5 percent, respectively.

What have we learnt so far? If we save $10,000 each year for 40 years until retirement, there is greater than 99 percent chance that we will have accumulated a value of $500,000, and most likely, we will have more than $1,000,000. With the high-risk investment, there is even a good chance that the accumulated value will be several million dollars.

We also see some of the same pattern as in an earlier section, that is, that for long horizons, the high-risk investments start to dominate. If the interest rates grow in future years or the investment period extends beyond 40 years, this domination would have been stronger yet.

Annual Investments Starting With $10,000 and Then Growing at 2 Percent Annually

It is realistic that our ability to save increases throughout our career as our salaries increase due to inflation and promotions. Thus, I have modified the annual investments to start at $10,000 and then increase by a modest 2 percent each year thereafter.

After 20 years, the low-risk portfolio value has a 99 percent confidence interval between $259,000 and $628,000, and the average is $409,000.

In comparison, the high-risk portfolio value has a 99 percent confidence interval between $215,000 and $1,337,000, and the average is $572,000. This is shown in Figure 9.4.

After 40 years, the low-risk portfolio value has a 99 percent confidence interval between $863,000 and $3,165,000, and the average is $1,692,000, while the high-risk portfolio value has a 99 percent confidence interval between $772,000 and $12,314,000, and the average is $3,518,000. Also, the probabilities that the values of the low-risk and high-risk portfolios exceed $1,000,000 are 96.1 and 96.8 percent, respectively. This is shown in Figure 9.5.

The next question is: How far does one million dollars take us in retirement? If one million is likely to be enough, we have found a way to

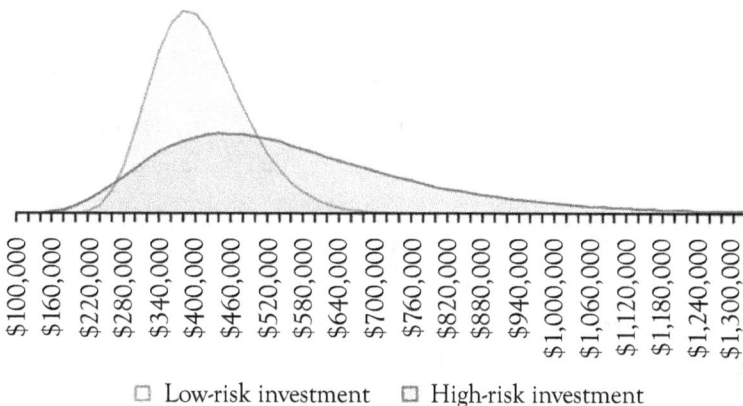

□ Low-risk investment   □ High-risk investment

Figure 9.4 Values after 20 years

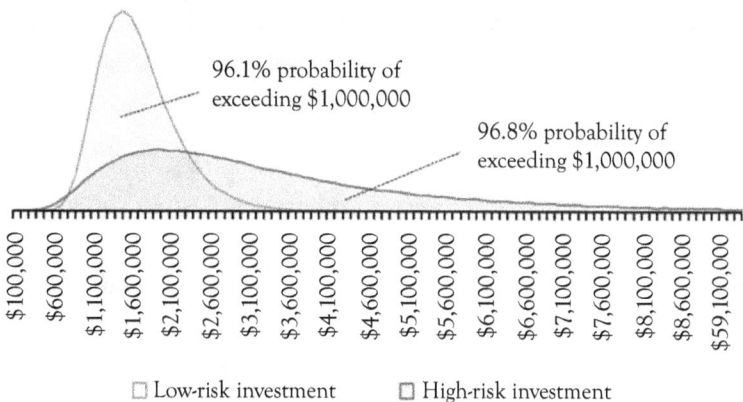

96.1% probability of exceeding $1,000,000

96.8% probability of exceeding $1,000,000

□ Low-risk investment   □ High-risk investment

Figure 9.5 Values after 40 years

get there, that is, invest $10,000 in the first year, followed by 39 years of 2 percent investment growth. But if we need more, say, $2,000,000, we should double the annual investments. That brings us to the next section, which examines the depletion of our investment during retirement.

Depletion of Wealth

In this section, I assume that we retire with a portfolio value of $1,000,000. Like earlier, the portfolios are either low or high risk. Furthermore, there is a mix of short-term investments (the funds that are withdrawn in early years) and long-term investments (the funds that are withdrawn in later years).

What is the *safe withdrawal rate*? That is, what proportion of the portfolio value can retirees withdraw each year without running out of money while they are still alive? Financial adviser William Bengen concluded in a 1994 article of the *Journal of Financial Planning* that a first-year withdrawal of 4 percent followed by inflation-adjusted withdrawals in subsequent years should be safe, meaning that the funds should last at least 30 years. This is often referred to as the *4 percent rule* and has been adopted as a common rule of thumb in the wealth management community (though some think it is too aggressive).

In the next two subsections, I examine two variations of the 4 percent rule. First, I set the annual withdrawals to 4 percent of the portfolio value in the beginning of each year, which allows for substantial year-to-year variations in the withdrawals but ensures that the funds never run out. Second, I set the first annual withdrawal to 4 percent of the portfolio value and then increase the withdrawals by 1 percent in each subsequent year, similar to what Bengen did in his original analysis.

Annual Withdrawals of 4 Percent

In this section, I examine a strategy of withdrawing 4 percent of the portfolio value each year. Naturally, as the portfolio value fluctuates, so will the withdrawals. In that sense, this strategy comes with great uncertainty in the annual withdrawals. Yet, it can be argued to be safer than a set withdrawal value because the withdrawals decrease when the portfolio value decreases, such that the funds never run out. My analysis, then, focuses on the withdrawal values in various years and not how long the funds last.

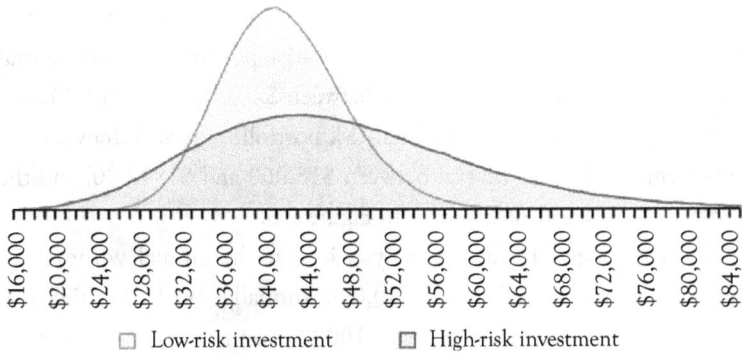

☐ Low-risk investment   ☐ High-risk investment

Figure 9.6 Withdrawal in year 5

Figure 9.6 shows the distributions of the value of the withdrawal in year 5 (i.e., five years after retirement). For the low-risk portfolio, the withdrawal has a 99 percent confidence interval between $29,000 and $56,000, and the average is $42,000. For the high-risk portfolio, the withdrawal has a 99 percent confidence interval between $23,000 and $82,000, and the average is $46,000. Thus, while the average withdrawals are decent, the lower values are getting uncomfortably low already in the fifth year, especially for the high-risk portfolio.

After 10 years, the distributions have widened further, but fortunately most of the additional variability occurs on the upper side. For the low-risk portfolio, the withdrawal has a 99 percent confidence interval between $26,000 and $69,000, and the average is $44,000. For the high-risk portfolio, the withdrawal has a 99 percent confidence interval between $19,000 and $131,000, and the average is $57,000. This is shown in Figure 9.7.

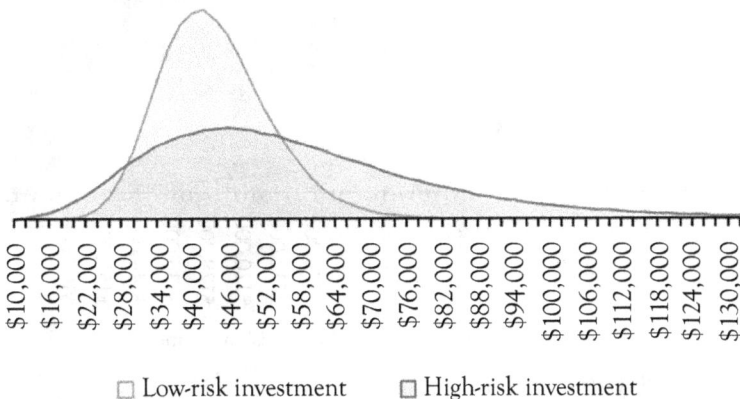

☐ Low-risk investment   ☐ High-risk investment

Figure 9.7 Withdrawal in year 10

After 15 years, the general pattern of higher average values and increased variability continues. For the low-risk portfolio, the withdrawal has a 99 percent confidence interval between $24,000 and $81,000, and the average is $46,000. For the high-risk portfolio, the withdrawal has a 99 percent confidence interval between $18,000 and $194,000, and the average is $69,000. This is shown in Figure 9.8.

The good news from the analysis is that the annual withdrawals are expected to be well above $40,000 annually. With the high-risk portfolio, they might even exceed $100,000 over time. The bad news is that the withdrawals might drop below $20,000 for the high-risk portfolio.

What do you think? Could you live with the possibility that the withdrawals might drop to $20,000? Of course, the answer depends on your living expenses and other sources of income. If you own your residence fully (so you do not have any mortgage payments) and receive, say $30,000, in social security benefits, you might be fine even if the withdrawals drop to $20,000. But for many, the possibility of lower withdrawals for the high-risk investment are unacceptable, in which case they should switch to safer investments upon retirement.

Based on this analysis, I would not recommend a withdrawal rate above 4 percent. Even 4 percent might be too aggressive, and you should consider 4 percent as the maximum withdrawal rate, with the objective of withdrawing 3 percent or less.

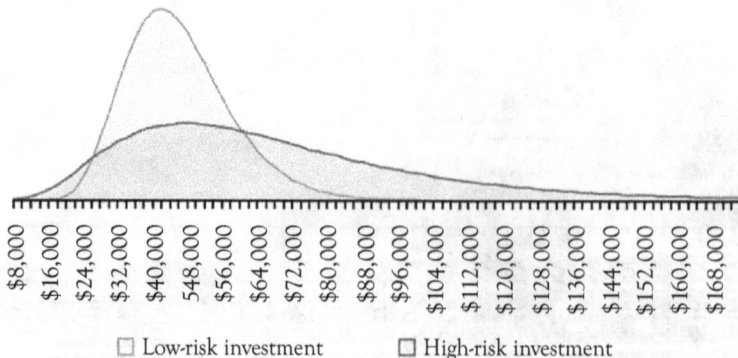

☐ Low-risk investment   ☐ High-risk investment

Figure 9.8 Withdrawal in year 15

Annual Withdrawals Starting at $40,000 and Then Growing at 1 Percent Annually

Let us alter our strategy to withdraw $40,000 (representing 4 percent) in the first year, and then increase the withdrawal amount by 1 percent each year to reflect a modest inflation.[3] Now the question becomes: How many years would the low-risk and high-risk portfolios last?

Figure 9.9 shows the distribution of the number of years of whole withdrawals (not counting partial withdrawals). There is a 100 percent probability that the low-risk portfolio would last at least 15 years and a 99.7 percent probability that the high-risk portfolio would last that long. The probabilities that the portfolios last 30 years drop to 94.5 percent for the low-risk portfolio and 93.3 percent for the high-risk portfolio. Thus, if you think you will live until age 100, there is a nontrivial chance that your investment account runs out.

If you are uncomfortable with the 6 to 7 percent probability of exhausting your portfolio in 30 years, the obvious answer is to withdraw less. If you only withdraw $30,000 in the first year, followed by annual increases of 1 percent, the probabilities that the portfolios last 30 years increase to 99.8 percent for the low-risk portfolio and 98.4 percent for the high-risk portfolio. Thus, if you want to make sure that you can rely

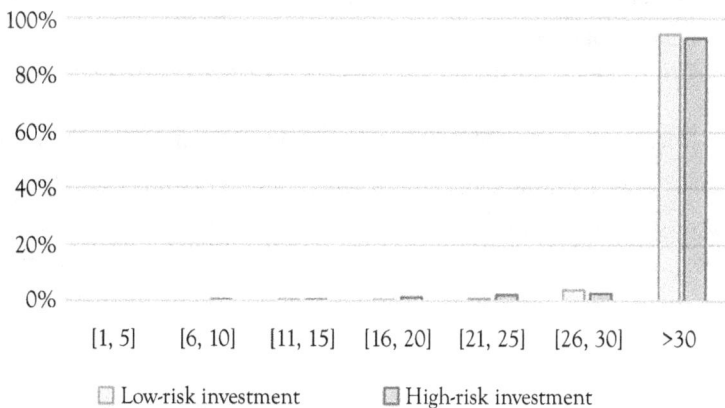

Figure 9.9 Years of withdrawals

---

[3] If your entire portfolio is in a non-Roth retirement account, you might be forced to withdraw more than $40,000 if the portfolio increases in value.

on withdrawals until you are a centenarian, you should select the lower annual withdrawals combined with the low-risk portfolio.

Life Expectancy

The simulations suggest that life expectancy is a key determinant of the suitable withdrawal strategy. According to statistics from the Social Security Administration, a 65-year-old woman (man) is expected to live to the age of 86 (83), while a 70-year-old woman (man) is expected to live to the age of 87 (85). These statistics, along with the earlier simulation results, are helpful in thinking about (1) when to retire, (2) how much you need to save for retirement, and (3) the withdrawal strategy during retirment.

However, there is great variability in actual life span, so it is useful to consider some distributions as well. The graphs in Figure 9.10 show the probabilities that men and women who are 65 and 70 years old live to various ages.

Thus, if you are a women who is retiring at age 65, there is a 14 percent chance that you will live for another 30 years until the age of 95. Alternatively, if you wait to retire until the age of 70, there is a 4 percent chance that you will live for another 30 years until the age of 100. Naturally, even these probabilities paint an incomplete picture, because they also depend on an individual's health and lifestyle.

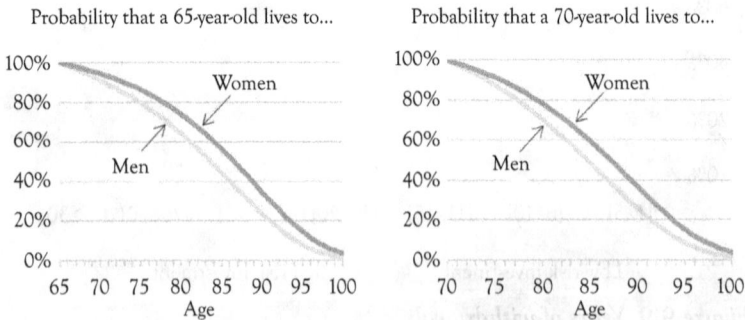

Figure 9.10 Probabilities of reaching various ages

In practice, two problems arise when individuals consider their life span in financial planning:

1. Many individuals focus on life expectancy and are oblivious to the possibility that they will live much longer. This possibility is often referred to as *longevity risk*.
2. Survey evidence suggests that individuals systematically understate the probability of living beyond the age of 75, perhaps by more than 10 percent. This phenomenon has been dubbed *survival pessimism*.

The oblivion to both longevity risk and survival pessimism could result in inadequate planning and raise the chance that the money runs out at an old age. Thus, we should always plan well beyond our expected life span to be on the safe side. Personally, I will make sure to be covered financially until I am at least 100.

CHAPTER 10

Estate Planning

At the end of our lives, it is likely that we still have significant assets in our possession (i.e., the estate), and most of us have a goal or intention for how those assets are to be distributed. For example, we might wish to donate significant assets to charities or pass the assets to family members. Estate planning, as illustrated in Figure 10.1, helps us achieve that in a timely, cost-efficient, and conflict-free manner.

The main objective for this chapter is to learn how the estate can be transferred with minimum conflict, court involvement and legal fees, and taxes.

Figure 10.1 Estate planning

Wills, Probate, and Bypassing Probate

Wills

A *will*, as shown in Figure 10.2, specifies how the estate should be distributed upon death. If you die *intestate*, that is, without a will, the state's intestacy laws apply. For example, in Iowa, the spouse inherits everything if you either have no children or children together, and the children inherit everything if you have no spouse.

There are several will types. A *holographic will* is handwritten and signed by the testator but not necessarily witnessed, and it is valid in most states but not in, for example, Iowa. An *oral (nuncupative) will* consists of declarations made by a testator who is about to pass away. The minority of states that accept them have additional requirements, including a minimum number of witnesses to the declarations and a maximum period by which the witnesses write it all down. Given the potential problems with the aforementioned types, you should either find a lawyer to make a typewritten will or do it cheaply online. Then you need to sign the document, find two or more witnesses who are not beneficiaries to also sign it, and, ideally, have it notarized (though most states do not require notarization).

Figure 10.2 Will

Probate

Probate is the legal process that validates the will or settles the estate according to the intestacy laws. It can be quite expensive, costing perhaps as much as 5 percent or more of the estate value, and it can delay the transfer of the assets, perhaps by a year or more. Also, the probate record (including the will, the estate inventory, and the identities of heirs) becomes part of the public record.

Fortunately, there are several ways in which we can bypass probate (often referred to as *will substitutes*), thus ensuring privacy and saving both time and money. Figure 10.3 illustrates, and the next subsections discuss these methods in greater detail.

Avoiding probate does not, however, affect estate taxes. Nor does it evade the claims of creditors; if there are insufficient assets to pay off debt, any assets passed outside of probate may be subject to creditors' claims.

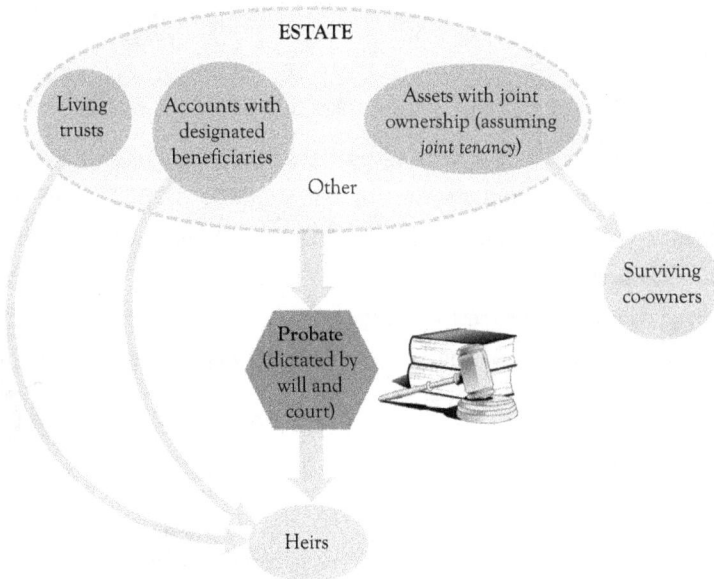

Figure 10.3 Bypassing probate

Beneficiary Designations

Regardless of whether you have a will, you should designate beneficiaries on your retirement accounts and life insurance policies. Beneficiary designations on these accounts override wills and, thus, bypass probate. If you are single, you can choose anyone as beneficiaries; if you are married, your spouse might have some rights unless (s)he signs a waiver.[1]

For assets other than retirement accounts and life insurance policies, you can often use payable-on-death (POD) or transfer-on-death (TOD) designations to assign beneficiaries and avoid probate. With simple paperwork, POD designations can be used for bank accounts and government securities, while TOD designations can be used for brokerage accounts. Increasingly, states also allow TOD registrations for motor vehicles and TOD deeds for real estate.

Why don't we take a 30-minute break here so you can look over your accounts to ensure that they have beneficiaries. If they already do, you can award yourself a well-deserved coffee break before proceeding to the next subsection.

Living Trusts

A *trust* is a legal entity that holds assets that an individual (the *grantor*) has "granted" and designates a trustee to manage those assets. A *living trust* is created while the grantor is alive, unlike a *testamentary trust*, which is created by a will. The beneficiaries (also called grantees) of a living trust receive the assets in the trust when the grantor dies. Like a will, the living trust dictates the grantor's wishes regarding the assets. But unlike a will, the living trust bypasses probate.

---

[1] For 401(k) plans and other plans subject to ERISA, a spouse is entitled to at least half of the account upon the owner's death, regardless of who is listed as the beneficiary, unless the spouse signs a written waiver during marriage. For IRAs (including 401(k) accounts that have been converted to IRAs) and other plans not subject to ERISA, a spouse has no legal right, except in the nine so-called community property states (including California and Texas), where a spouse has the right to 50 percent of the assets contributed during marriage.

A downside to a living trust is that it usually costs at least $1,000. However, like with wills, there are online tools that can help reduce the cost substantially. Another downside is that a living trust requires assets to be retitled and transferred to it, which can be a hassle.

If the living trust is *revocable*, you can change or revoke the trust as you wish. You can name yourself to be the trustee while you are still alive, but you also need to name a successor trustee, like a trusted family member or friend, to manage the assets if you become incapacitated or die.

If the living trust is *irrevocable*, you relinquish all control and interest in the assets of the trust. Thus, the assets are safe from creditors and lawsuits, and they are no longer part of your taxable estate (though transfers to the trust are generally subject to gift tax). It even pays its own taxes on any earnings.[2]

Overall, living trusts can be a useful tool to avoid probate, which is valuable in states with high probate costs and for individuals with substantial assets subject to probate, especially if those assets suffer in value when stuck in probate court for a prolonged period. Furthermore, irrevocable versions can be useful for individuals susceptible to lawsuits and might even reduce estate taxes for the very wealthy.

Joint Ownership

Assets, including cars, real estate, and bank accounts, can be owned jointly. For example, if a couple acquires a house, it is common for both individuals to become owners, as in Figure 10.4.

There are two main categories of joint ownership, *joint tenancy* and *tenancy in common*, and the owners are often referred to as tenants.[3] The two categories differ in the required ownership terms and in what happens to the property when one owner dies.

---

[2] An irrevocable life insurance trust (ILIT) can be used to hold your life insurance policy. The trust becomes the policyholder, paying the premium on your behalf and distributing the death benefit to the beneficiaries. The structure circumvents both estate taxes and the probate process.

[3] In some states, individuals who are married to each other often take title in *tenancy by the entirety* instead of *joint tenancy*, but there is little practical difference.

Figure 10.4 Joint ownership

With *joint tenancy* (also known as joint tenant with the right of ownership), two or more individuals own assets jointly and in equal proportions, and when one passes, ownership transfers automatically to the surviving owner(s). The automatic transfer to the survivors is called the *right of survivorship*, and it bypasses both probate and any will. This ensures a swift and costless transfer of ownership.

With *tenancy in common*, two or more individuals also own assets jointly, but when one passes, the ownership becomes part of the estate and subject to the will and probate. In other words, there is no right of survivorship. There is also no requirement for the owners to hold equal stakes in the property.

Joint tenancy is an effective and common strategy for avoiding probate. But there are some caveats. First, any common ownership can become problematic if conflicts between the owners arise. Second, the assets are subject to probate when the last owner dies unless that owner employs some other strategy like a living trust. Third, one owner could sell her ownership to a third party or transfer her ownership as *joint tenant* to *tenant in common,* and in both cases, the joint ownership changes to tenancy in common.

Relevant Taxes

Estate Taxes

The *estate tax* (also cleverly dubbed "death tax" by its opponents) is levied on the estate after death but before transfer to beneficiaries, so it is

Figure 10.5 Estate taxes

essentially paid by the deceased, as Figure 10.5 illustrates. The federal estate tax is progressive and ranges from 18 to 40 percent, where 40 percent applies to taxable amounts above $1 million. In addition, states can levy a separate estate tax (though, e.g., Iowa does not).[4]

While the estate tax sounds hefty, there is a substantial exemption that I discuss later so that most estates avoid estate taxes entirely. Thus, there is no reason to panic just yet.

Gifts and Gift Taxes

A gift is a transfer of property to other individuals while getting nothing, or less than full value, in return. Such gifts, as exemplified in Figure 10.6, are subject to *gift taxes*, which we will see work together with estate taxes.

However, there are important exemptions. First, direct payments to medical and education providers are excluded. Second, the federal gift tax has a $17,000 per year exemption in 2023 *for each giver and for each gift recipient*. Figure 10.7 shows historical annual gift exemptions. Thus, if a married couple gives each of their three kids up to $17,000 × 2 = $34,000 in 2023 for a total of $34,000 × 3 = $102,000, the gifts are exempted. If you give a single person more than $17,000 in 2023, you must file IRS

---

[4] Iowa is one of a few states that also has an inheritance tax paid by the beneficiaries in the range of 5 to 15 percent, but it does not apply to reasonably close relatives, which obviously include children of the deceased.

Figure 10.6 Monetary gift

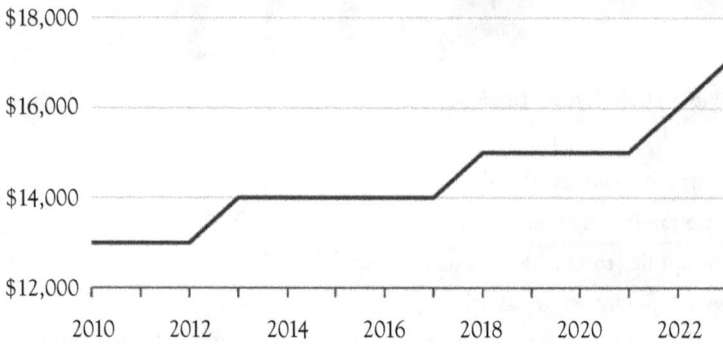

Figure 10.7 Historical annual gift tax exemptions

Form 709, and the excessive amount counts toward your lifetime exemption and will be taxed along with the rest of the estate at the estate tax rate if you also end up exceeding the lifetime exemption. (See more on the lifetime exemption later.)

Contributions toward a 529 college savings plan for, say, a grandchild, is also treated as a gift. But they have a slight edge to other gifts: you can contribute five times the annual limit in one lump sum of $85K (in 2023) and still qualify for the exemption, but then you cannot contribute during the next four years without exceeding the exemption. That allows the money to grow tax-free longer inside the 529 plan.

Generation-Skipping Transfer Taxes

The purpose of the unified gift and estate transfer tax system is to ensure that the transferor pays the same taxes on transfers of property during life (gifts) and at death (bequests). The *generation-skipping transfer (GST) tax* is imposed on transfers to grandchildren and more remote descendants that exceed the exemption limits, so that the transferors cannot avoid transfer taxes on the next generation by "skipping" a generation. This closes the loophole where inheritances could skip a generation to avoid double estate taxation.

I should clarify, though, that the annual exclusion of $17K (as of 2023) also applies here, so you can still give sizeable and regular gifts to your grandchildren without paying GST taxes.

Lifetime Exemption

Finally, we are getting to the so-called lifetime exemption, which ends up saving most estates from taxation. In 2023, the gift, estate, and GST tax exemption for a U.S. citizen or resident is **$12.92** million. That means that an individual can transfer property with value up to the exemption amount either during her lifetime or at death without paying any transfer tax.

Let me illustrate with an example. Suppose that Leon has gifted each of his two daughters $150K every year for the last 10 years (i.e., from 2014 to 2023). He also covered one daughter's medical expenses of $350K, but those gifts are excluded. Then the tax exemptions are: $14K × 2 × 4 (for years 2014 to 2017) + $15K × 2 × 4 (for years 2018 to 2021) + $16K × 2 × 1 (for 2022) + $17K × 2 × 1 (for 2023) = $298K, and the lifetime taxable gifts equal ($150K × 2 × 10) – $298K = $2,702K. The remaining exemption amount that could be used by Leon's estate upon his death is $12.92 million – $2.702 million = $10.218 million. If Leon's estate is valued at $12 million upon death, $12 million – $10.218 million = $1.782 million is subject to taxation. Figure 10.8 illustrates this.

You might ask the following then: If you are likely to exceed the lifetime exemption, should you gift early or wait? That probably depends on issues beyond taxes, such as the needs of your children. But if you aim to minimize taxes, you should start by giving the maximum exempted value annually to each of your intended beneficiaries (like your children) and perhaps to each of the children of your beneficiaries (like your grandchildren). You might even gift more, given that the money would otherwise grow in your account, thus increasing the total taxable amount. As a secondary concern, you should probably hold on to stocks

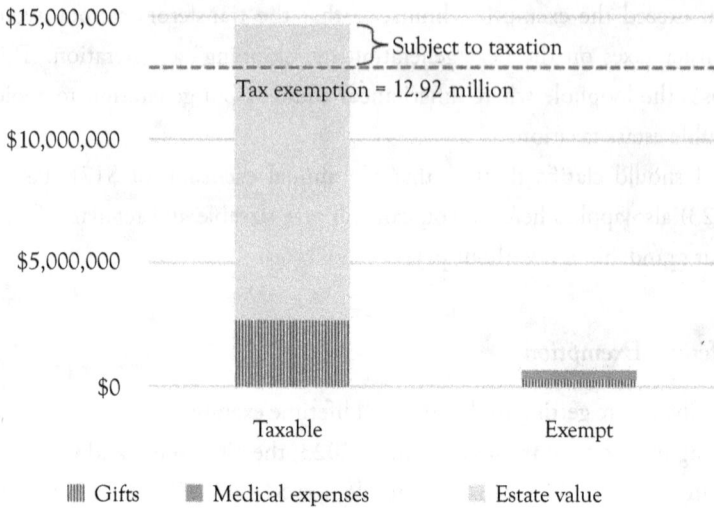

Figure 10.8 Leon's estate example

with large capital gains because their cost basis carries over for gifts, but it is reset at death. That way, you can save your beneficiaries from some capital gains taxes when they sell the stock.

The current estate and gift tax exemption law sunsets in 2025, meaning that unless Congress acts in the interim (which is likely), the lifetime exemption is scheduled to be cut in about half in 2026. But the IRS left a loophole—it has ruled that beginning in 2026, the estate tax threshold will be the greater of (i) the prevailing exemption, likely to be around $6 million, and (ii) the total taxable gifts made during life, up to the value of the old exemption. Thus, elderlies with large estates should consider gifting up to the lifetime exemption value in 2025, thus effectively dodging any large drop in the exemption starting in 2026.

Unlimited Marital Deduction and Portability of Lifetime Exemption

The unlimited marital deduction allows unlimited tax-free transfers to a U.S. citizen spouse any time, even at the death of the transferor. Furthermore, the lifetime exemption is portable between spouses, meaning that the deceased spouse's unused exemption (DSUE) transfers to the surviving spouse. To make the portability election, the decedent's estate

Figure 10.9 Married couple Brian and Denise

must file an estate tax return (Form 706) within nine months of death, even if the estate would not otherwise be required to file.

Suppose that married couple Brian and Denise in Figure 10.9 have given taxable gifts of one million dollar each. If Brian were to die in 2023, his estate could be transferred tax-free to Denise. Furthermore, if the estate files a timely estate tax return and elects portability for the DSUE, the DSUE of $12.92 million – $1 million = $11.92 million would transfer to Denise. When Denise dies, her estate could use Denise's exemption (which would depend on the exemption in the year of her death) along with the DSUE from Brian. Incidentally, there will be no reduction or claw back of the DSUE if the exemption is reduced in the future.

Available Deductions From Gross Estate

I should also note some available deductions that can be made from the gross estate when estimating the value that is potentially subject to estate taxes. First, as noted earlier, property that passes to the U.S. citizen surviving spouse is deducted as marital deduction. Second, property left to a qualifying charity is deducted, essentially giving you a last chance for a tax-deductible donation. Third, as you probably already assumed, mortgages and other debt are deducted. Finally, administration expenses of the estate are deducted.

Treatment of Retirement Accounts

General Guidelines

As I recommended earlier, you should designate beneficiaries for each of your accounts to avoid probate. Upon your death, the full value of your account balances will be transferred to your beneficiaries, and the entire value is included in the value of the estate for estate tax purposes, unless the beneficiary is the surviving spouse. Any deferred income taxes will continue to be deferred until withdrawals are made.

If the beneficiary is a surviving spouse, the account can simply be rolled into the surviving spouse's account (even if this account is brand new), assuming that the types of account are the same (i.e., both are traditional or both are Roth). This might be beneficial if the surviving spouse is younger because the RMD is then based on the age of the surviving spouse. If the deceased's account is a traditional IRA or 401(k), the surviving spouse can convert it to a Roth IRA in the name of the surviving spouse, but the conversion value is subject to income taxes. The surviving spouse can alternatively transfer the assets to an Inherited IRA. The RMD is based on the age of the surviving spouse, but the initial distribution depends on the age of the deceased spouse; if the deceased spouse was older than 73, the surviving spouse must start taking RMDs the following year, otherwise the RMDs can be delayed until the deceased spouse would have turned 73.[5] This might be beneficial if the surviving spouse is older than the deceased spouse and the deceased spouse died before age 73.

If the beneficiary is a nonspouse, the beneficiary may not simply transfer the assets into his or her account. The only option is to transfer the assets to an Inherited IRA (unless the beneficiary disclaims the

---

[5] Moreover, with an Inherited IRA, the RMD is based on the IRS Single Life Expectancy Table, which assumes a shorter life expectancy than the Uniform Life Table.

assets, of course). The 2019 SECURE Act then requires the assets to be withdrawn within 10 years, though there are some beneficiaries who may be allowed to stretch the payments over their life expectancy, including (i) minor children of the deceased, (ii) those who are less than 10 years younger than the deceased, like most siblings are, or (iii) those who are disabled or chronically ill.

If you inherit an IRA, I strongly recommend you investigate these issues more closely and perhaps even consult with an attorney or tax adviser because there are lots of details, exceptions, and even uncertainties in the regulations. For example, financial advisers commonly interpret the SECURE Act to mean that that an Inherited IRA account must be emptied by the end of the 10th year after death, but proposed new regulations would specifically require annual withdrawals to avoid stiff penalties.

Concept Test—Designating Beneficiaries on IRA and Roth IRA Accounts

Ruth lost her husband several years ago, and she is now wondering whom to designate on her IRA and Roth IRA accounts. She has two children: Sarah, who is a 45-year-old social worker, and Isaiah, who is a 42-year-old investment banker. What should Ruth do?

Let us assume that Sarah has a lower employment income tax rate than Isaiah. Then, from a pure tax-perspective, Ruth should designate Sarah as the beneficiary on the IRA account because withdrawals from that account are subject to income taxation, while Isaiah should be the beneficiary on the Roth IRA account because withdrawals from that account are tax-free.

If the two accounts have the same values, Ruth should also consider giving Sarah more of her other assets for two reasons. First, on an after-tax basis, the traditional IRA account is less valuable, even with Sarah's low tax rate. Second, Sarah's income potential is smaller, so she is likely to benefit more from the assets.

What if both children were investment bankers with substantially higher tax rates than Ruth? Then Ruth should consider converting the funds from the traditional IRA account to the Roth IRA account at her low tax rate so that Sara and Isaiah do not have to pay taxes on the funds that they inherit. Furthermore, Ruth should do this little by little so as not to push her income into a high tax bracket.

Concept Test—What Accounts to Tap First in Retirement

Married couple Liz and Dave are both 66 years old, healthy, and retired. They have three million dollars spread equally across an IRA account, a Roth IRA account, and a regular brokerage account, as illustrated in Figure 10.10. Which account should they tap first to cover their retirement expenses?

They probably receive social security benefits, perhaps $20,000 annually. Furthermore, they are required to withdraw roughly $40,000 annually from their IRA account when they turn 73, on which they must pay employment income taxes. If they need more funds, the conventional wisdom is that they should withdraw from their regular brokerage account first, then the IRA account, and, lastly, the Roth IRA account. This allows the funds to grow longer in tax-free accounts and preserves the RMD flexibility in the Roth IRA account.

However, there are another couple of considerations. First, Liz and Dave likely have more than enough assets to cover their retirement and might plan to leave some assets to their heirs. In that case, it might make sense to leave securities with substantial capital gain in their regular brokerage account because of the step-up in the basis that occurs upon the death of the couple. This allows the heirs to sell these securities tax-free, whereas Liz and Dave would have to pay capital gains taxes when selling them. Second, because tax rates are progressively higher for higher

Figure 10.10 The three accounts of Liz and Dave

incomes, it makes sense to even out the taxable income across the years. That means that the couple should convert some funds from their traditional IRA to the Roth IRA every year, at least in the years before the RMD kicks in at the age of 73. And if they need to make a large withdrawal from one of the IRA accounts in a year, for example, to purchase a property, they should consider using the Roth IRA account for a bulk of it to avoid being pushed into a high tax bracket.

To supplement the social security benefits and RMD withdrawals, I would recommend Liz and Dave to first sell securities in the regular brokerage account that have a combined zero net capital gain or, perhaps better yet, a $3,000 net capital loss that they can deduct against their income. When they exhaust that possibility, it is unclear whether they should sell securities in the regular brokerage account with capital gains or withdraw more than the RMD from one of the IRA accounts. That depends on the magnitude of the capital gains (both those that have already occurred and those that are expected to occur), their life expectancy, their tax rates, and even the tax rates of their heirs, and I will not try to optimize further here.

Epilogue

In an online chat in 2013 with personal finance author Helaine Olen, University of Chicago professor Harold Pollack argued that the best financial advice can fit on an index card. In response to demand for such a card, he quickly made one and posted a picture of it online. The picture went viral and was even picked up by major newspapers. Based on this success, Olen and Pollack later coauthored a book that elaborated on the principles in the index card.

Figure E.1 reproduces Pollack's index card. I fully agree with it, except his advice never to buy or sell an individual security. Pollack's reasoning for avoiding individual securities is that you are unlikely to be able to consistently identify under- or overvalued securities, so there is no use trying. I agree. But I believe that a portfolio of individual securities offers valuable flexibility that funds lack, which I showed in an earlier chapter.

> Harold Pollacks' simple financial advice:
> - Max your 401(k) or equivalent employee contribution.
> - Buy inexpensive, well-diversified mutual funds such as Vanguard Target 20xx funds.
> - Never buy or sell an individual security. The person on the other side of the table knows more than you do about this stuff.
> - Save 20% of your money.
> - Pay your credit card balance in full every month.
> - Maximize tax-advantaged savings vehicles like Roth, SEP and 529 accounts.
> - Pay attention to fees. Avoid actively managed funds.
> - Make financial advisors commit to the fiduciary standard.
> - Promote social insurance programs to help people when things go wrong.

Figure E.1 Harold Pollack's index card

Inspired by Pollack's index card, I decided to make one based on this book. A key difference, though, is that I first wrote most of this book and then the card, whereas Pollack first wrote his card and then a book. Anyway, Figure E.2 shows my card.

A summary of advice based on this book:

- Contribute the maximum possible toward your retirement accounts. Also consider Roth accounts to elevate the maximum.
- Invest in a diversified portfolio. Much of it can be low-fee index funds, but also invest in individual securities for added flexibility in your non-retirement accounts, e.g., to harvest losses.
- Invest primarily in stocks, especially if you have an investment perspective of at least 10-20 years.
- Only sell what you have bought if you desperately need liquidity or when you periodically harvest losses.
- Get health insurance + term life insurance when you have dependents.
- Get college savings accounts for your kids/grandkids.
- Count on less than 4% annual withdrawal from retirement accounts.
- Designate beneficiaries to accounts to avoid probate.

Figure E.2 Index card based on this book

If you follow this advice, you should be in solid financial health when you retire. In the meantime, stay calm despite great volatility in your life and the stock market, as in Figure E.3.

Figure E.3 Staying calm in the midst of volatility

APPENDIX

Simulating Portfolio Values

This appendix shows how you can simulate and present future portfolio values using the embedded functions in Excel. Even if you do not fully understand each step below, you can construct your own simulation by replicating the Excel content.

Step 1

I first created a spreadsheet that calculates the value of a portfolio at the end of each of 10 years, as depicted in Figure A.1. The input variables include:

- The expected return of the portfolio per year (set to 8 percent in cell B3);
- The standard deviation of the portfolio returns per year (set to 14 percent in cell B4);
- The beginning value (set to $30,000 in cell B5); and
- The annual investment, which is assumed to occur at the beginning of each year (set to $5,000 in cell B6).

The annual return is assumed to follow a normal distribution with an average equal to the value in cell B3 and a standard deviation equal to the value in cell B4. To do this in Excel, I wrote =NORM. INV(RAND(),B3,B4), where RAND() is a random value from a uniform distribution between 0 and 1, and NORM.INV() transforms the uniform distribution to a normal distribution with the given average and standard deviation.

I am primarily interested in the portfolio value after 10 years in cell D19. Each time I recalculate the spreadsheet, the portfolio value is simulated to be a new value. In the trial in Figure A.1, the portfolio value happened to end up at $169,908.

	A	B	C	D
1	**Simulation of portfolio value**			
2				
3	Expected return	8.00%		
4	Standard deviation	14.00%		
5	Beginning value	$30,000		
6	Annual investment	$5,000		
7				
8	Year	Investment BOY	Return	Value EOY
9	0			$30,000
10	1	$5,000	9.76%	$38,414
11	2	$5,000	19.04%	$51,681
12	3	$5,000	-11.31%	$50,269
13	4	$5,000	-10.02%	$49,730
14	5	$5,000	11.47%	$61,008
15	6	$5,000	4.46%	$68,953
16	7	$5,000	26.53%	$93,576
17	8	$5,000	27.05%	$125,240
18	9	$5,000	19.30%	$155,380
19	10	$5,000	5.94%	$169,908

	A	B	C	D
1	**Simulation of portfol**			
2				
3	Expected return	0.08		
4	Standard deviation	0.14		
5	Beginning value	30000		
6	Annual investment	5000		
7				
8	Year	Investment BOY	Return	Value EOY
9	0			=B5
10	1	=B$6	=NORM.INV(RAND(),B$3,B$4)	=(D9+B10)*(1+C10)
11	2	=B$6	=NORM.INV(RAND(),B$3,B$4)	=(D10+B11)*(1+C11)
12	3	=B$6	=NORM.INV(RAND(),B$3,B$4)	=(D11+B12)*(1+C12)
13	4	=B$6	=NORM.INV(RAND(),B$3,B$4)	=(D12+B13)*(1+C13)
14	5	=B$6	=NORM.INV(RAND(),B$3,B$4)	=(D13+B14)*(1+C14)
15	6	=B$6	=NORM.INV(RAND(),B$3,B$4)	=(D14+B15)*(1+C15)
16	7	=B$6	=NORM.INV(RAND(),B$3,B$4)	=(D15+B16)*(1+C16)
17	8	=B$6	=NORM.INV(RAND(),B$3,B$4)	=(D16+B17)*(1+C17)
18	9	=B$6	=NORM.INV(RAND(),B$3,B$4)	=(D17+B18)*(1+C18)
19	10	=B$6	=NORM.INV(RAND(),B$3,B$4)	=(D18+B19)*(1+C19)

Figure A.1 Step 1 of spreadsheet

Step 2

Now we need to repeat the simulation in the first step enough times to form a reasonably smooth distribution. With designated simulation tools, we could readily set the number of trials to a million. With only the basic Excel tools, I limit the trials to 5,000. To trick Excel into recalculating 5,000 times and storing the value from each trial, I use *Data Table* in Excel. First, I went to cell G2, which will be the top of the data table, and inserted =D19. Then I highlighted the area F2:G5001, selected *Data Table*, inserted E1 (or any other cell) as the *Column input cell*, and pressed OK. This is shown in Figure A.2.

	F	G
1	**Trials using Data Table**	
2	1	$169,908
3	2	$136,282
4	3	$81,218
5	4	$66,199
6	5	$125,759
7	6	$85,229
8	7	$118,074
9	8	$74,301
10	9	$114,236
11	10	$221,197
12	11	$114,114
13	12	$130,045
14	13	$99,756
15	14	$141,860
16	15	$148,718
17	16	$154,762
18	17	$93,255
19	18	$141,656

	F	G
1	**Trials using Data Table**	
2	1	=D19
3	2	=TABLE(,E1)
4	3	=TABLE(,E1)
5	4	=TABLE(,E1)
6	5	=TABLE(,E1)
7	6	=TABLE(,E1)
8	7	=TABLE(,E1)
9	8	=TABLE(,E1)
10	9	=TABLE(,E1)
11	10	=TABLE(,E1)
12	11	=TABLE(,E1)
13	12	=TABLE(,E1)
14	13	=TABLE(,E1)
15	14	=TABLE(,E1)
16	15	=TABLE(,E1)
17	16	=TABLE(,E1)
18	17	=TABLE(,E1)
19	18	=TABLE(,E1)

Figure A.2 Step 2 of spreadsheet

Step 3

Lastly, I need to create a histogram. The quick and easy way in Excel is to highlight the data in column G, select *Insert > Chart > Histogram*, and then alter the formatting to your liking.[1]

I will instead focus here on an alternative way that is more elaborate but provides more flexibility in how the histogram appears. First, I need to count the number of portfolio values that fall in various ranges (called bins) so that I can make a histogram. Figure A.3 shows this counting process. In cells J4 to J7, I calculated various percentiles to get a sense for the width of the overall distribution of portfolio values. Cell J10 estimates a possible bin size that I could use by dividing the difference between the 1st and 99th percentiles by 30 (which is a reasonable number of bins). I ended up choosing a minimum value of $50,000 (which is a bit lower than the first percentile) and a bin size of $10,000 for my histogram, and I inserted those values in cells J13 and J14.

Column L contains the lower values of each bin based on my choices in cells J13 and J14. Column M counts the number of portfolio values that fall in each bin using a specialized count function in Excel. I simply wrote =FREQUENCY(G:G,L:L) in cell M3, where G:G refers to column G that contains the 5,000 portfolio values and L:L refers to column L that

	I	J	K	L	M
1	Histogram				
2	Average	$143,347			Count
3	Percentiles			Less	4
4	1%	$63,189		$50,000	24
5	5%	$78,520		$60,000	92
6	95%	$233,771		$70,000	157
7	99%	$298,331		$80,000	240
8				$90,000	362
9	Diff 1% vs 99%	$235,142		$100,000	432
10	Rough bin size	$7,838		$110,000	484
11				$120,000	448
12	Use these			$130,000	443
13	Minimum	$50,000		$140,000	409
14	Bin size	$10,000		$150,000	370
15				$160,000	296
16	# less than min	4		$170,000	249
17				$180,000	230
18				$190,000	148
19				$200,000	135

	I	J	K	L	M
1	Histogram				
2	Average	=AVERAGE(G:G)			Count
3	Percentiles			Less	=FREQUENCY(G:G,L:L)
4	0.01	=PERCENTILE(G:G,I4)		=J13	
5	0.05	=PERCENTILE(G:G,I5)		=L4+J$14	
6	0.95	=PERCENTILE(G:G,I6)		=L5+J$14	
7	0.99	=PERCENTILE(G:G,I7)		=L6+J$14	
8				=L7+J$14	
9	Diff 1% vs 99%	=J7-J4		=L8+J$14	
10	Rough bin size	=J9/30		=L9+J$14	
11				=L10+J$14	
12	Use these			=L11+J$14	
13	Minimum	50000		=L12+J$14	
14	Bin size	10000		=L13+J$14	
15				=L14+J$14	
16	# less than min	=COUNTIF(G:G,"<"&J13)		=L15+J$14	
17				=L16+J$14	
18				=L17+J$14	
19				=L18+J$14	

Figure A.3 Step 3 of spreadsheet

---

[1] On a PC, you can right-click on the horizontal axis and select *Format Axis*. Then you can select a round value at about the first percentile for the underflow bin, a round value at about the 99th percentile for the overflow bin, and a reasonable bin width. On a Mac, you need to instead click on a column, right-click and select *Format Data Series*, to get to similar options.

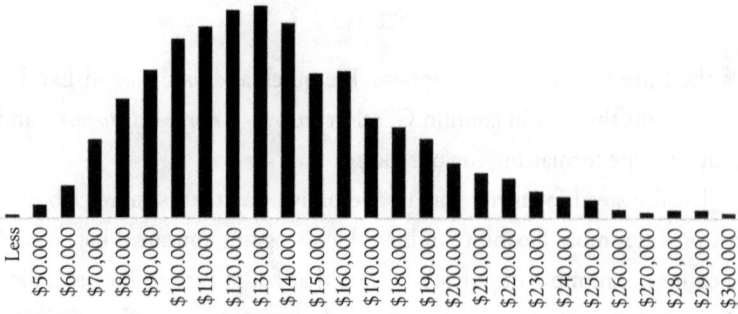

Figure A.4 Histogram of simulated values

contain the lower values of each bin. Excel then automatically filled in the rest of the counts.[2]

Based on columns L and M, I made the histogram in Figure A.4 by highlighting cells L2:M29 and selecting *Insert > Chart > Column*.[3] Recall that column L contains the lower value for each bin, so we should interpret the bar that says, for example, $50,000 as portfolio values starting at $50,000 to the beginning of the next bin, that is, $60,000.

---

[2] An alternative is to use the COUNTIF function, which does not automatically fill down. For example, to count the number of observations less than the value in cell L4, I could write =COUNTIF(G:G,"<"&L4).

[3] I could also use a line graph here, which is especially useful when displaying several distributions in the same graph as I did in Chapter 9.

About the Author

Erik Lie is the Amelia Tippie Chair in Finance at the University of Iowa. He has published widely in top academic journals and has been recognized by *Time* magazine as one of the 100 most influential people in the world. In recent years, he has developed and taught courses on wealth management and served as an expert witness in lawsuits related to financial advising.

Index

Note: Page numbers followed by f and t refers to figures and tables respectively. Page numbers followed by "n" refer to footnotes.

OTHER TITLES IN THE FINANCE AND FINANCIAL MANAGEMENT COLLECTION

- *Mastering Options* by Philip Cooper
- *The Corporate Executive's Guide to General Investing* by Paul Mladjenovic
- *The Human Factor in Mergers, Acquisitions, and Transformational Change* by Muhammad Rafique
- *Understanding Cryptocurrencies* by Ariel Santos-Alborna
- *Understanding the Financial Industry Through Linguistics* by Richard C. Robinson
- *Sustainable Finance and Impact Investing* by Alan S. Gutterman
- *The Non-Timing Trading System* by George O. Head
- *Small Business Finance and Valuation* by Rick Nason and Dan Nordqvist
- *Finance for Non-Finance Executives* by Anurag Singal
- *Blockchain Hurricane* by Kate Baucherel
- *Risk Management for Nonprofit Organizations* by Rick Nason and Omer Livvarcin
- *Conservative Options Trading* by Michael C. Thomsett
- *Understanding Behavioral BIA$* by Daniel C. Krawczyk and George H. Baxter
- *Valuation of Indian Life Insurance Companies* by Prasanna Rajesh
- *Understanding Momentum in Investment Technical Analysis* by Michael C. Thomsett
- *Trade Credit and Financing Instruments* by Lucia Gibilaro

Concise and Applied Business Books

The Collection listed above is one of 30 business subject collections that Business Expert Press has grown to make BEP a premiere publisher of print and digital books. Our concise and applied books are for...

- Professionals and Practitioners
- Faculty who adopt our books for courses
- Librarians who know that BEP's Digital Libraries are a unique way to offer students ebooks to download, not restricted with any digital rights management
- Executive Training Course Leaders
- Business Seminar Organizers

Business Expert Press books are for anyone who needs to dig deeper on business ideas, goals, and solutions to everyday problems. Whether one print book, one ebook, or buying a digital library of 110 ebooks, we remain the affordable and smart way to be business smart. For more information, please visit www.businessexpertpress.com, or contact sales@businessexpertpress.com.

www.ingramcontent.com/pod-product-compliance
Lightning Source LLC
Chambersburg PA
CBHW061217220326
41599CB00025B/4665